Lawrence Bohme Publications 2020

Montefrio, Down Through Time

written and illustrated by
Lawrence Bohme
known in the region as "Lorenzo"

A la memoria de Manolo, pastor, carnicero y cantaor

An artistic, historical and human portrait of the town of Montefrio, in the western hills of Granada Province, Andalucia, followed by the author's stories about his life there over the years.

Dear visitor,
It may seem strange that an Englishman should be the author of the only guidebook to an Andalucian town. In fact, I have lived here much longer than I ever did in England, and in many ways feel myself to be an adopted son of this half-forgotten bit of Spain, of which I have the honour of being the first and for many years only foreign resident. I first came here as a student in 1960 to hear the great flamenco singer - may he rest in peace! - Manolo Avila. As you can imagine, I fell in love with the singer, the music and the town, and many years later, tired of wandering, I bought a farmhouse nearby and decided to stay.

3

Speaking several languages, I established myself as a free-lance interpreter, working at conferences throughout the region. Some years later I had the idea of making it possible for other curious travellers to enjoy the life of this farming town with its many relics of the past, its traditions and its welcoming people. I purchased first one and then another peasant cottage, made them comfortable and got started in the very new "rural tourism" business.

Since there was no guidebook, I wrote one myself, to give my guests an idea of some of the many pleasant and interesting things to see and do in Montefrio. At first it was just a sheaf of photocopies stapled together with a drawing on the first page, which went from hand to hand. Then I was asked to make a real book out of it in English and Spanish, with illustrations by our local photographer. Roads and Trails of Montefrio allowed me to describe some of the finds I had made in the archaeological site, to help us better understand how the local people lived between the long Roman period and the Moorish invasion of 711.

But once the Internet came of age, I found myself restoring other cottages to take care of more curious travellers. And once I got to work on my Montefrio book, I decided to add new elements, such as a guide to the archaeological site. With the advent of young people from Spain's cities wishing to stay in their hitherto shunned boondocks, to use the American expression, I translated my book into Spanish under the title, Montefrio por los siglos, *or "Montefrio over the centuries".*

Until quite recently, few "outsiders", foreign or Spanish, ever strayed this far from the beaten path, partly because they didn't know it existed and partly because there was nowhere to stay once they got here. All we were famous for was our spectacular church on the ruins of the Arab fort on the cliff, and, as one popular British guide book belatedly says, our truly delicious - if you are partial to blood sausage - "black pudding". But I am sure that once the reader has gazed up at the former and bitten into a chunk of the latter, he or she will soon discover that there is much more to Montefrio than its spectacular old church and succulent morcilla...

A short history of Montefrio

It is not strange, in the light of Andalucia´s agitated history, that the village of Montefrio should have changed place twice since it was created, each time moving westward, from one mountain roost to the other. The first settlement began 7,000 years ago on a crag facing the Sierra de Parapanda, and it was there that the Roman colonizers discovered it. After the fall of the Empire it shifted to another, equally impregnable height nearby, and it reached its third and final perch, several miles west overlooking the valley of the Milanos River, at the end of the Dark Ages, 500 years later.

First came a prehistoric tribe, which settled on the heights of a natural fortress called Los Castillejos. Its people were Iberian shepherds and buried their dead in massive stone tombs, or "dolmens".

Much later, the Romans subdued the natives and had them live below on the fertile plain of the Parapanda Valley to grow wheat. The Romans produced flour in a series of six ingeniously designed mills using the scant water of the creek, the Arroyo de los Molinos, to supply the cities of the region and perhaps Rome itself.

When Hispania fell to the semi-barbarians called the Visigoths, the people of the valley - who lived in the Roman way and practised Christianity - continued to lead their peaceful existence of shepherds and farmers, far from the struggles between Visigothic princes and bishops, royal cousins and brothers, which raged constantly in Toledo and Granada.

But another foreign invasion, by the Byzantines, who wanted to reconquer the Empire which their Roman forefathers had lost, forced the community to once more seek refuge in the hills. This time they chose an outcropping of stone which, like an island, could be easily defended and had a spring of water at its feet, now called Castillón Hill.

Scarcely a century later, the Byzantines gave up their nostalgic undertaking and sailed back to Constantinople. After a short interval, the Moors invaded Spain in turn and settled, among other parts of the peninsula, on the plain of Granada. The *Montefrieños* up on their hilltop held tight, becoming one of the many Christian enclaves which survived in Andalucia... until the tribes of warring Moors, finally united under the Caliphate of Cordoba, forced the them to disperse and become part of the mainstream society...

The new Moorish lords of Montefrio chose to build their outpost on the summit of a third and more impregnable promontory several miles to the west, which became the nucleus of the current town. When the Castilian Reconquest reached this part of Spain in the mid-14th century, effectively placing the tiny outpost on the constantly challenged northern frontier, the Moors were forced to build a larger castle. This obstacle, along with the civil wars and popular revolts which then immobilized the Christian enemy, enabled the Moors' garrison in Montefrio to hold firm until the final dissolution of their Spanish kingdom, a century and a half later.

After the Christian Reconquest, the town was repopulated with people from northern Spain who, with no internal enemies to fear, chose to live more comfortably at the foot of the great cliff, rather on the plateau. The village grew and became a farming town with several fine churches. The oldest of these, which was built on the ruins of the Moorish castle, is known today as the "iglesia de La Villa".

Two great churches, and a Moorish castle

Our stroll - or climb, if you wish - will take us backward through time, since we are going to begin in the Plaza with the relatively modern *Iglesia de la Encarnación*. It is said to be the only perfectly round church, having a smooth stone dome without ribbed supports, in Spain and even in the world. It was designed towards the end of the 18th century in the neo-classical style of the French Enlightenment, by a fashionable Madrid architect, Ventura Rodriguez, who never came here himself and is better known for the church of Santa Fé, the town near Granada which Isabel and Ferdinand built as a camp from which to command the siege of the Alhambra. Ventura also designed the Cathedral of Pamplona, and several other churches in the "Kingdom of Granada" as the reconquered territory was called until the end of the 19th century, including those of the neighbouring villages of Algarinejo and Alomartes.

Although this church is not especially beautiful - in an irreverent frame of mind, I once likened it to a pressure cooker - it is very impressive when seen from afar. Inside, the lack of effective windows creates a distinctively gloomy atmosphere, like a planetarium without stars. In line with the church's neo-classical style, it was meant to be a scaled-down imitation of one of Rome's most famous monuments, the Pantheon of Agrippa, with its vast dome.

There are two differences though. The Pantheon has an open source of light in the middle – the *oculus*, or eye – which illuminates everything from above. Also, its dome was made of cast concrete, using the Roman invention of today's modern cement. But in the chaos which followed the fall of the Empire, the formula for the cement "that was stronger than stone" was lost, seemingly forever. For well over a thousand years all buildings needing concrete had to make do with traditional and crumbly mortar, until the British rediscovered how it was made in the early 19th century, naming it "Portland cement".

[We do not often realize it, but other great Roman structures, such as the Coliseum and the Pont du Gard aqueduct in southern France, were also made of poured concrete but esthetically sheathed afterwards in stone. Had they been of stone only, they might well have collapsed under their own weight!]

The stone dome of Montefrio, like many other things here, has a mystery all of its own. Since no records of the construction were kept, we don't know how such a gigantic bulb could be created without the use of scaffolds, which would have required a forest of timbers that was nowhere around. The most convincing explanation is that once the vertical drum was built it was filled with sand and rubble. The roof stones were then fitted on top of this great cake so perfectly that once the filler was removed they formed a perfect dome. Vast numbers of peasants were attracted from the countryside to do the work, not – it is said – for a daily wage but because, as the level of the filler rose, foremen scattered gold coins all about the surface. Once done, the same workers were allowed to frenetically shovel out the earth and keep for themselves any coins they found ...

With this modernistic building campaign, the intention of Spain's enlightened monarch, Charles III, was to shed the light of 18th century humanism on the region's backward and superstitious folk countryfolk, which explains the disconcerting lack of decoration. The aim was to create a new Andalucian man, in line with the progressive ideas of the time, and although religion was not yet rejected outright, it was firmly relegated to second place after Reason.

The hundreds of swallows' nests under the eaves of the dome have been there for so long that they're now a symbol of the village in their own right, always forming a halo around pictures of our Madonna, the Virgin of the Remedies, who is enshrined here. This pretty statue of the Mother with Child seems to have been manufactured in Italy, in spite of the legend which claims she was miraculously found in a trunk during a storm. She still means so much to the villagers that when, in the Civil War, a brigade of anti-clerical Republican soldiers set about breaking up effigies in Montefrio's churches, one of the conscripts, who was a native of the village, managed to hide her in the neighbouring convent, where she was kept until the fighting was over. As the sole survivor of the iconoclastic deluge, every August 15th – the "day of all madonnas" - she is dressed in her finest robes and solemnly paraded around the town, making even the most anti-clerical Montefrieño's heart swell with pride.

Another well-loved legend says that the Bishop of Granada came to see the statue after she was discovered in the trunk and found her so beautiful that he insisted she be installed in the cathedral. But as soon as the cart which carried her away reached a certain point the mules refused to go any further, so she was allowed to remain in Montefrio. It is a measure of the villagers' devotion that the particular spot where the mules balked is still known as *El Tranco*, the barrier.

All the other paintings and statues in the church are replacements installed after the Civil War, gaudy store-bought articles. The only precious object beside the Lady is the pulpit, to the left of the altar, ornately carved in pink marble, which makes it clash with the austere surroundings. The pulpit originally belonged to the church on the cliff, and having spent a good deal of money on it the villagers decided to take it with them when the damaged church was abandoned. The irony is that, with its rococo style, the pulpit was too sophisticated in style for the old church, and too fussy and old-fashioned for the new one, making it esthetically out of place in both.

After the Civil War, Franco had large memorial crosses nailed to churches such as this one, with the names of those villagers who had been "wickedly murdered by the Marxists" - *vilmente asesinados por los marxistas* - painted on black wooden panels. When I returned to Montefrio in 1983, after an absence of twenty years, I was surprised to discover that the new Communist mayor had removed ours only a few weeks before. Curiously, the workers, with that indifference to detail which is so dismayingly Spanish, failed to sand or blast away the pale shadow which the cross left on the gingery brown stone, so that for many years later it hung there like a ghost, reminding those who knew it of harder times.

The broad street to the left of the church, which heads up toward the castle, is curiously (although not officially) known as *La Plaza Alta*, the High Square, and the first building on the left is our tourist information office, housed in an ancient and elegant building called the *Casa de Oficios*, or Guild Hall. When I first stayed in Montefrio the small building was our post office and so thickly coated in plaster and whitewash that no one suspected it was in fact a priceless relic. After the post office was moved to its present location and the decrepit market building which stood in front of it had been demolished, the mysterious façade was cleaned and restored, and identified as a 16th century assembly room for the town's business guilds and craftsmen.

Next we come to the *Ayuntamiento* or Town Hall, an 18th century palace which once belonged to the Valdecasas family who sold it to the Town Council in 1945. Just above it stands a former church, the *Ermita de San Sebastián*, on the street of the same name. This chapel was built in the 16th century and expropriated by the State in the 19th, having been used for various purposes since then, until recently as our Health Clinic. We are still hoping that, as promised, it will become our long-dreamed of archaeological museum.

The alleyway which separates these two buildings is called the *Calle del Muro*, the Street of the Wall, because the outer wall of the old Moorish fort once ran through this part of the village. We climb on, passing on our right the very steep Calle Santiago, so named for a penniless schoolteacher who lived there at the beginning of the 20th century. He was greatly admired by the villagers who fed him in exchange for the lessons he gave to their children and, after his death, they had the street renamed in his memory.

We continue up the Calle de San Sebastián, and come to a belvedere which overlooks the picturesque quarter called La Solana, famous for its gypsy community. In Spain, where the winters can be dank, any place which receives the sunlight from dawn to dusk is called a *solana*, or sunny spot.

11

To our right we see the profile of one of the Moorish towers which protected the cliff's southern slope.

Now we swerve about and climb an even steeper street, until we come to a small, asymmetrical square, or *plazuela*. This quarter, at the foot of the castle, is called El Arrabal, an Arabic word which means "outlying area". If you turn sharply to the left and walk along the path, you will see the strange cave-like houses which are built against the cliff, most of which are uninhabited.

Lying just outside the fortress (hence its name), this is the most ancient, although uninhabited, part of the town.

La Villa, castle and church

Returning to the plaza, cross to the far end and turn left to the castle gate. As you walk up the steps under the towering cliff and church, notice the crumbling remnant of masonry on the right, standing on its own like a jagged claw. This is all that remains of the Moorish military gate which once arched overhead to join the cliff. Compared to the foundations of the church on our left, the Moorish masonry is crude, composed of an outer shell of rough, squarish stones and a filler of clay and smaller stones called *argamasa*.

The Reconquest reaches Montefrio

How, one might ask, did such a great church come to be built in such an inaccessible place, and on the ruins of an even greater fortress?

Shortly after the Moors swept through the peninsula in 711, the Christians, who had taken refuge in the mountains of northwestern Spain, began the 800-year long series of battles and truces called the Reconquest, during which they slowly pushed the enemy further and further south. This seemingly endless process culminated in the Moors' final expulsion – and the unification of Christian Spain – with the taking of Granada in 1492.

The Christian crusade reached this part of Andalucia in the mid-14th century, after King Alfonso XI took the Moorish port of Algeciras, cutting off the main link with the enemy's rear base in North Africa. Taking advantage of the Moors' disarray, he seized a string of castles to the north of Granada, including Alcalá de Benzaide, a place which he renamed Alcalá la Real ("royal") and is just 10 miles from Montefrio. The Moors of Granada responded by fortifying the new frontier with a series of fortresses, forming a crescent stretching across the bottom of the peninsula. In Montefrio, they built a massive castle, designed by the same architect who helped fortify the Alhambra.

During the century and a half in which this military outpost held, it suffered constant raids and skirmishes from the marauding Christians, aimed at taking booty and demoralizing the enemy. But when the quarrelling kingdoms of Christian Spain were finally unified with the marriage of Isabel of Castile and Alfonso of Aragon, forces were joined to drive the Moors from Spain forever. When the new Christian alliance reached the gates of Montefrio, in 1486, its coming inspired such fear that the siege laid was a mere formality. The castle's *alcaide*, or governor, is said to have begun negotiating surrender even before the invaders camped in front of the walls, on the meadow still called "La Real" – the Royal Meadow.

Once Montefrio was taken the well-worn routine was followed: 28 Christian captives were freed from the dungeon, the Moorish inhabitants were allowed to take refuge in Granada, and the town was repopulated with Christian immigrants. And as soon as Granada itself fell, the Alhambra's new masters built a series of monumental churches – such as our *"iglesia de La Villa"* – on the sites of the castles of their defeated enemies, as a symbol of their victory over Islam…

The large, elegant church we discover on the plateau is the product of a peculiar marriage of styles known as "Gothic-Renaissance". As such, it is a rare example of the merging of medieval and Renaissance architecture. When the building was designed in 1505, by the famous Granada architect Diego de Siloë, the new classical style and humanistic ideas were rejected by the Court of Castile because they were less passionately religious than the spirit of the Middle Ages, as seen in its great cathedrals.

Queen Isabel herself was a pious and austere Franciscan and insisted that all churches be built in the majestic late Gothic style which she had made famous in Toledo, and which we can see here in the ceiling with its intricately ribbed arches. But Isabel's successor and grandson, *Carlos Quinto*, was a "modern", which explains why the decorative columns, capitals and doors of our church, which was not completed until well into his reign, are Renaissance in style.

The remains of a small fortress stand behind the church, with crumbling walls perforated by loopholes and a mound of earth in the middle, as well as a deep-water cistern, once covered by an arched roof. We believed that this was a vestige of the original Arab fort, but historians now tell us that it was built shortly after the conquest in 1486 as a symbol of Christian lordship over the territory. Unfortunately, it had to be torn down a decade later due to the royal ban on fortresses in the region, aimed at discouraging internal conflicts.

It would seem, from the care with which the walls of the church and fortress were joined together, as well as the discovery of skeletons buried in the patio, that the remains of this short-lived fort later became Montefrio's first Christian graveyard.

The name of the church has a political significance which tells us much about the Reconquest and its aftermath. Like most of the churches in the reconquered territory it was dedicated to the incarnation of the spirit of Jesus in Mary's womb, *Iglesia de la Encarnación*. Accordingly, the scene carved above the door shows God overlooking a praying Mary and sending down to her, in the form of rays of light, the spirit of her son, with its explicit reference to her virginity. In the ideological battle between Christianity and Islam, the Christians felt that their trump card, so to speak, was the fact that their prophet had been born to a virgin, whereas Mohammed had a normal mother. So they constantly drove this point home to encourage, with disappointing results, the conquered Moors to embrace the True Faith.

This supposed "superiority" over Islam had much to do with the launching of the medieval cult of the Virgin Mary, which reached its climax in Spain with the stirring songs of Reconquest propaganda called the *Cantigas de Santa Maria* (the King Alphonse the Wise, who may have written some of them, insisted they be in Portuguese, which he felt was a more poetic language than Spanish). These several hundred polyphonic narratives were designed to uplift the morale of the Christians and undermine that of the Mohammedans. In one of them, for example, a Moorish woman whose son is ill desperately watches him sinking towards death, until, seeing a Christian woman praying before a statue of the Virgin Mary, she imitates her and her son´s health is restored.

Inside, the church is bare of all decoration, having been abandoned a few decades after the year 1767, when a lightning bolt struck the roof. It is said that when the church was struck, it was full of people praying, but only a dog who happened to be there was killed by the falling stones. This was considered a miracle which is still celebrated on the last Sunday of May with a holiday known as the *Día del Rayo*, the Day of the Bolt, when a solemn procession is led through the town by the priest and the mayor.

There is even a tradition that dogs can enter any church in the village, supposedly out of gratitude towards the four-legged victim for drawing the disaster upon itself, but, more pragmatically, in the hope that if another bolt strikes, the "miracle" will be repeated. I once put this to the test by allowing my pooch Bolinha to follow me inside the round church on the plaza, and not one of the pious ladies there moved to reprimand me.

The hole, barely a few yards across, was still there when I first came to Montefrio, with the rubble heaped together on the floor - after two long centuries! Manolo took me up on one of my first visits to hear him sing in the gutted nave because, he said, he liked the priestly resonance it lent to his voice…

One can assume that the villagers took advantage of the accident as a pretext for giving up the church altogether. Under the Moors the village had been perched on the plateau for defensive reasons, but once Spain became entirely Christian and there was no more fear of internal enemies, the new 16th century town spread more comfortably below, leaving the old Reconquest church stranded on the cliff. This effectively forced the faithful to climb all the way up the hill to Mass several times a day - an act of penitence in itself! So it stands to reason that they were delighted to have a new church, the current Iglesia de la Encarnación, built down below. During the half century between the Day of the Bolt and the completion of the new (round) church, they worshipped at the Ermita de San Sebastián, which we saw next to the Town Hall.

It may seem strange that the Christians – or original Spaniards – felt the need to fortify the town at all, since the Moors were soon subjugated everywhere. But, during the whole 16th century, the new "Kingdom of Granada" as the reconquered region was known was heavily militarized.

The Alhambra castle itself was reinforced with many up-to-date improvements - such as round rather than square towers, which latter were too vulnerable to the new artillery being used then - and walls of solid masonry rather than rubble-and-mortar.

All this due to the fear of civil uprisings among the old Moors, who had been falsely promised tolerance for their religion and customs in exchange for surrendering. The growing bitterness culminated in a bloody civil war half a century later, after which the old Moors – even if they had converted - were all expelled…

But the greatest threat came from the Turks of the Ottoman Empire, who having finally become the masters of Constantinople felt ready to sail their powerful fleet against southeastern Spain. Desperate pleas for rescue came from Granada's beleaguered *moriscos*, but the Turks never responded. Instead, they preferred to raid the closer and richer coasts of Provence and Catalonia, carrying away booty, and prisoners of high rank who could be exchanged for ransom…

A rebel Prince becomes King, in Montefrio

Being a frontier or border post and only half a day's ride from Castilian Spain, Montefrio (or *Muntefrid*, as the Moors called it) was an ideal base for the Alhambra's many palace plotters, since it was never difficult to enlist the Christian enemy's assistance in bringing down the current Sultan. The farcical story of Prince Ibn Ismael is a good illustration of the intrigues and cross-alliances which were rife throughout the Reconquest, slowly but surely allowing the Castilians to "divide and conquer".

In 1445, after the Sultan known as "Mohammed the Lame" seized power in Granada, the rebellious Abencerraje clan staged an uprising aimed at putting an ally of theirs on the throne, Prince Ibn Ismael, who was living in exile in... Castile, at the court of King Juan II, no less! The Moorish Prince obtained his royal host's backing and, heavily escorted by Christian knights, set off from Alcalá la Real's great fortress, the "Castillo de la Mota", to meet the leader of the Abencerrajes in Montefrio, where they were in league with the local commander. There, on the cliff overlooking the village, Ibn Ismael was proclaimed King of Granada.

When the Prince approached Granada at the head of an army massively reinforced by Christian troops, the "lame" Sultan, unable to muster popular support since his subjects were glad to see the end of his despotic rule, fled the Alhambra and allowed the pretender to take power.

However, Ismael was soon dethroned in turn, because the mistrustful *Granadinos* feared his "special relationship" with the Christians. Admittedly, this inglorious ending removes some of the luster from what some of my friends believe to be Montefrio's claim to historical fame, but I make a point of mentioning him here, for fear of being taken to task by the local patriots.

Why is the church on the cliff called "La Villa"?

For a long time, when I was a flighty youth, I was unable to find out why everyone in Montefrio calls this extraordinary site overlooking the t own "La Villa"... until I discovered the reason in a history book.

After Isabel and Ferdinand took Montefrio, they gave it the official status of a "town" rather than just a farming village or hamlet, officially naming it "Villa de Montefrio". Their first concern was to attract as many Christian settlers as possible, and Montefrio being a *"villa"* brought with it a number of administrative privileges, making life in the isolated place less difficult economically. And that is why, ever since, the townsfolk have fallen into the habit of calling the rock mountain, and specifically the ancient church, "La Villa".

Montefrío in Toledo

In the choir of the Toledo Cathedral, each of the magnificent walnut-wood stalls is carved with the Christians' seizing of the Moors' fortified towns during the War of Granada at the end of the 15th century. One of these grand seats is inscribed, in Gothic script, with the name "Montefrio", as you can see in this dramatized scene of the event, showing the enemy streaming out of the castle gate and declaring subservience to the proud knights.

On the right, a herald is announcing the victory with trumpet raised high... The carvings were commissioned – during the very bloody 10-year long war – by Queen Isabel's confessor, the legendary Cardinal Mendoza, who personally took part in some of the sieges. Alonso Berruguete, the leading sculptor of the Spanish Renaissance, was put in charge of the sumptuous carvings.

The view from the steeple

Now for the 111 steps of the bell tower, which will literally be the culminating point of your Montefrio experience! Fortunately there are several balconies and chambers to rest in on the way up. At the top of the steeple, we see that the bells disappeared long ago and that the roof is entirely new - when I first came here, there were no tiles on the church at all and the steeple was uncovered, giving it a flat-topped appearance.

The numbers crudely painted in black paint on the stones of the bell tower date from the late 1950's, when an earthquake destroyed the steeple, and the stones were numbered, arch by arch, before being reassembled. In 1984, another lightning storm destroyed half of the steeple again, and after it was rebuilt a lightning rod was attached to the side of the belfry.

The main tower of the Moorish fort stood here, so the view which the sentinels had must have been very similar, although somewhat lower, to the one from the steeple. *Muntefrid* – being what the Moors called "the left eye of the Alhambra" - had its own early warning system composed of a string of four *atalayas*, or watchtowers in the surrounding hills, which alerted the inhabitants of approaching enemy troops by means of flashing mirrors and smoke signals.

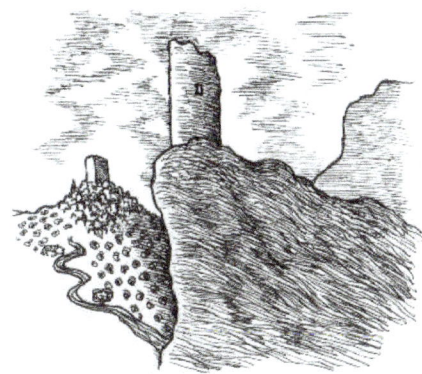

The first of these towers, on top of the Sierra de Parapanda (thoughtlessly destroyed to make way for the TV transmitter) overlooked the road leading south from the Christian fort of Moclín, the "right eye of the Alhambra" and main launching point for raids into the Moorish realm of Granada. From this tower the signal was relayed to three others (the ruins of one can be seen from the road to El Tocón and the other two are near the cemetery) until it was received by the castle.

The tower in this fanciful drawing is the one closest to Montefrio, or what's left of it... My little poem says, *In the green olive grove on the hill there is a Moorish watch tower, as golden-dark as your peasant girl's face…*

Various theories exist explaining the extraordinary shape of the great sandstone cliff, which resembles a gigantic slice of freshly cut gingerbread. The most common one is erosion, but a geologist who stayed in my houses thought it was caused by a split in the earth's crust, because we can see how, on the other side of the valley in which the town is sunk, the granite cliff facing it has a similar shape. Yet others claim that the cavity was, during the Ice Age, slowly torn out by a glacier, although it's very hard to imagine such a thing in parched Andalucia!

The "new" Montefrio

Looking north on the other side of the ravine, we see the "new" Montefrio, which took root in 1967 with the construction of the town's first public school. Before then, the only education was provided by the nuns who taught infants and a few wandering teachers, but things began to change in 1959, the year before I first came here. Franco's regime, anxious to improve its social image, sent a group of students from the University of Oviedo in the north to carry out a summer literacy campaign among the local *campesinos* - countryfolk.

I had an eyewitness account of this encounter of two different worlds from our *señorito* or country squire Don Curro, owner of the Torre del Sol olive oil mill. Being an incorrigible rake my friend Curro was intrigued by the students' arrival mainly because most of them were young women from well-off families. He rode right over on his horse to gallantly invite them – as he did

Lilo and me - to have a dip in his swimming pool, which then and for years to come was the only *piscina* worthy of the name in Montefrio.

Whilst admiring the comely *señoritas'* fashionable swimsuits, still the old belly-covering kind (rather than the *dos piezas* or bikini which was forbidden on the beaches, with all the shameless *francesas* desperate to undress) he heard with great amusement, as a semi-feudal landlord himself, how shocked they were by the backwardness and ignorance which they found among the peasantry. The *cortijeros* were kindly to them, but the girls, all city dwellers, never got used, among other things, to breakfast being just a chunk of bread and a swig of anis at sunrise…

[I should add that Curro himself never to my knowledge bathed in his pool. As a proud Spanish gentleman he would never have dreamed of being seen in his underwear, but instead sat comfortably in the shade, attired in his well-pressed trousers and shiny shoes, sipping a glass of sherry while his *invitadas* disported themselves under his admiring gaze…]

After these up-and-coming ladies went back home, they complained about their Spartan summer so publicly that Montefrio soon became synonymous with misery, creating much embarrassment in the halls of power. I learned of the outcome from our Mayor Don Pepe Guzmán – also known as "Pepe Flores" because he planted geraniums in every empty space in town, most spectacularly on the slope as you come down from the bridge, where they still flourish...

"All I had to do was catch the train to Madrid and visit the right *politico* and the next day we got the long-promised funds for building a school!", he cackled. Pepe was a member of the Falange Party which appointed him Mayor (no elections then) but well-liked by the villagers, especially for planting all those geraniums which were not only beautiful but also prevented hillsides from being washed away by the rain.

Pepe – who was no longer the Mayor when I returned to Spain - also thought highly of this book, after his son, while taking a world cruise, was asked by the Spanish-speaking clerk at a hotel in Hong Kong what place in Spain he was from. When the boy proudly answered, "a small town called Montefrio", the Chinese hispanophile jumped up in surprise. "I have read a book about Montefrio!" he cried, "and it's by an Englishman who calls himself Lorenzo!". That was my consecration, at least in that particular ex-Mayor's eyes, as an international literary success.

To the right of the school, the long rows of semi-detached bungalows are low-income "council" housing. The yellow wheat silo nearby was built soon after the Civil War to assure bread supplies in case of shortages, but it was never used, perhaps because very soon the farmers gave up wheat farming for more profitable "export" crops such as olives.

At the very end of the new district is the public swimming pool, one of the biggest and best-appointed in the region. Incomprehensibly to foreign visitors, it's only open during the summer school holidays, end of June to mid-September. The reason for this is, like so many other things, a cultural one: Andalucians cannot conceive of jumping into the water unless the weather is very, very hot.

23

Further on is the factory where by the local farmers have their olives milled, the "Cooperativa San Francisco de Asis". A look around confronts us with the unavoidable fact that we are surrounded by a sea of olive trees. Since this is a plant we aren't familiar with in our countries, even though we're exceedingly fond of its juice, I have added this story I wrote for a magazine about the olive oil industry. I hope it will answer some of the questions that visitors usually ask when gazing around in awe at the scene...

What's in an olive?

As you travel along the mountain road, the white village which appears below in the valley, with its towering castle-church, resembles a ship sailing across a rolling sea of bushy, low-lying, gnarled trees... those trees that produce the green gold which all the world desires. Montefrio's olive oil is known for its purity and pungent flavour. In fact, much of the highly reputed and expensive Italian-brand olive oil which is sold in New York in those pretty golden tins is the product of our groves, cleverly shipped across the Med and packed for re-export by the descendants of Machiavelli.

The main difference between the quality of olive oil and wine is that fermentation improves grapes but damages olives, which means that the best oil comes from very fresh olives that reach the mill soon after being picked. The oil which is produced by the first pressing is known as virgin, or extra virgin, depending on the quality of its smell and taste. Just go into any coffee shop and order the Andalucian equivalent of a slice of bread and butter, *una tostada con aceite*, which is a toasted roll over which you generously sprinkle the glorious liquid along with a pinch of salt, and savour it for yourself.

From Roman times up to the first half of the 20th century, olives were crushed between millstones that were turned by hand, pushed by river water or dragged by animals. In the 19th century a steam-powered system was invented which began with the crushing of the fruit under three large conical stones, a system which, although now largely superseded, is still used in some mills, powered by electricity. The tip of the cone of each stone was attached to an axle and a complex system of gears rotated the base of the stones so that they rolled over the olives. The system was until recently still used by the Molino de San Cristóbal, and not long ago one was reconstructed to decorate a traffic island in Montefrio, on the northern edge of town.

The juice is then extracted from the crushed olives by means of a vertical press composed of two iron plates at either end of a shaft several meters high. Round straw mats called *capachos*, woven with a circular hole in the middle, are placed over the shaft one by one, after a layer of crushed olives is poured between them. When pressure is applied on the upper plate, this multiple sandwich is compressed and the oil which oozes out from the mats is collected in a pan below.

Our other mills use modern Italian-made stainless steel equipment, which crushes the olives between rollers and then separates the resulting mash, diluted with warm water, by centrifugal spinning. The three elements which result from the milling process are oil, fiber (called *orujo*) and a very bitter substance called *alpechin*. When foreigners come to Spain for the first time they invariably make the mistake of picking a fat, shiny olive and biting into it, to the delight of the locals, who point the way to the nearest fountain so that the gagging victim can rinse out his mouth. When olives are cured for eating rather than oil, and left in a solution of briny water, this substance is slowly released and rises to the surface where it can be skimmed off, like a black, malodorous scum.

The disposal of the *alpechin* or "vegetable water" is a major nuisance in Spain, not only because it stinks - especially in summer - but because it fouls farm wells. After the oil has been removed from the fibrous *orujo*, the remaining sawdust-like substance is used for heating fuel and for baking bricks and ceramics, but no one has yet devised a convenient way of recycling the unwanted *alpechin*. The ponds you see in the countryside, full of black liquid (or the dried remains thereof) are where the unwanted substance is dumped. These ponds, or *alpechineras*, are now supposed to be a minimum distance from inhabited areas, in spite of which one can often smell the ponds in the outskirts of olive-farming villages such as ours.

All oil produced in Montefrio is top-grade virgin for the simple reason that we do not have a *refinería*. The fibrous *orujo*, or, in English, "pomace", is taken to the big refineries in the outskirts of Granada. If you are here during the harvest, in wintertime, you will notice trucks leaving the village loaded with what appears to be lumpy wet soil. You can see huge mountains of it in front of the oil factories when you pass by Sierra de Elvira, on the way into town. There, chemical solvents are used to extract all the remaining oil from the fiber.

This "refined" oil, called *aceite de orujo* or *orujillo*, is much blander in taste and paler in colour, and of course commands lower prices. If you buy *aceite virgen* in the grocery stores, you will usually see in the small print that it is in fact *virgen* blended with *aceite de orujo*, in the same way that old wines are blended with new. But ours is guaranteed 100% virgin - in any case, Montefrio has no factory able to chemically process the fiber.

[It should be recalled that in times past olive oil was often avoided because of its strong taste and acrid smell. Foreign travellers, and especially the French ones hated eggs fried in it and longed for butter instead, there being few cows about didn't exist. The streets of Montefrio at noon were redolent with the stench, I recall when I first came to Montefrio, and it took some getting used to. But then, technology came along with centrifugal filtering machines to remove the *alpechin* which miraculously made of olive oil the most exquisite thing you could cook in, sprinkle of salad and even your morning toast.]

The value of virgin oil is mainly determined by the percentage of *acidez*, or "acidity", created by oxidation. Olives which have been blown off the tree by wind or picked some days or weeks before milling will have fermented, which causes greater decomposition of the amino acids than in olives which are milled immediately. However, prompt milling is not the only way of preventing spoiling. The proper handling and washing of the olives, and correct cleaning and fumigation of the trees, are also important.

Most of the oil milled in Montefrio has a low "acidity" rate of 0.4%. When the level of acid breakdown in the olives reaching the mill is too high, they must be sent to the refinery, like the residual *orujo*. That is why each mill is equipped with its own testing lab. The denomination "extra virgin" - in Spanish, *virgen extra* - can only be given by an official taster from the *Instituto de la Grasa* in Seville, to oil with, as well as low acidity, exceptionally good flavour, colour and odour.

At a typical modern mill, such as the *Cooperativa de San Francisco*, the process is as follows: the olives are dumped from the truck into a bin, from which they are fed by conveyor belts to machines which remove the leaves and twigs and wash them clean. Then they are crushed and processed, as described above. The extracted oil must stand for several months in huge vats so that any remaining solid particles can sink to the bottom, before being sold.

It takes roughly 5 kilos of olives to produce a liter of olive oil, depending on the quality and ripeness of the fruit, and the farmers either take away the agreed amount of oil for their own use, or sell the olives to the mill. But since most farmers only require a small amount of oil for their own use, the large part of the total crop is sold for cash. Rising prices on the international market, due to olive oil's high standing with nutritionists, has touched off a real "olive fever", with new trees being planted everywhere, usually in the place of almond trees and cereals (although now, with the recent health craze for almonds, this trend is being reversed...). A tree can produce between 50 and 150 kilos of olives, and it takes about 8 years for a newly-planted sapling to begin bearing fruit.

Many visitors to Spain believe that green olives and black olives are grown on different varieties of tree, but in fact the green ones are unripe olives which are picked early, in October. The picking of green olives for eating purposes is called *verdear*, or "greening", and, being largely for local consumption, only concerns a tiny percentage of the total production. In Spain, the custom is to use green olives for eating and black ones for oil only, even though foreigners, such as myself, often prefer them "Greek style".

Most olives, therefore, are left to ripen and turn black, until late November or early December when they can be picked for milling. The harvesters work in teams - *cuadrillas* - of four or five; the men use long sticks to beat the branches - *varear* - and the women spread huge nets - *mantas* (once made of canvas, nowadays of nylon mesh) under the tree and gather the olives which fall into it. Since the terrain is mountainous, the edges of the lower part of the net are propped up with stakes, to prevent the olives from bouncing downhill.

But the windfalls must be picked off the ground by hand first, which means that more women are needed when the winter has been stormy than when all the fruit has stayed on the branches. This is why, when the winter has been calm, the village women can be heard to lament that "this year they won't have much need of *mujeres*".

The soil of the olive groves is tilled constantly and herbicide is used to prevent grass from taking hold, because the farmers believe that this aerates the roots and encourages permeation of rainfall. However, it also facilitates wind erosion, and agronomists complain that this, along with over-planting, is turning Spain into "a desert with olive trees", and when you fly over it that is certainly the impression you get. In some traditional regions like Extremadura the olive groves are also used for growing grapes on the ground between the trees, which is not only beautiful to behold but not, as far as I know, detrimental to the total yield.

[In all fairness to our over-zealous *cortijeros*, it should be said that the stripping of Spain's vegetation began long ago with the ancient Romans, who cut down most of the dense forests which covered the peninsula to smelt ore from the mines they dug here, since copper and tin and iron were, for them, the country's most precious asset. It is even claimed that before the Romans arrived, a squirrel could make its way from Gibraltar to the Pyrenees through the treetops without once having to touch the ground, if you can believe that!]

Since the heavily ploughed surface is rough, a few months before the olives are ripe (when they are most likely to fall) a circular space under the tree is smoothed with rakes, or by a battery of truck tires dragged by a tractor, to make it easier to collect them manually. This is called *hacer el suelo* - "preparing the ground" - and is the reason for the peculiar beach-like appearance of the land under the trees.

After the harvest, the trees are pruned of all the older branches because they are less productive, a job which is an art in itself. In Spain, the olive trees are not allowed to grow to more than 3 or 4 meters in height as they are in Italy and France. The trunks are constantly cut down to just above ground level, to allow new branches to sprout from them, so that although some of the trees may be centuries old, their branches are always new. The current trend is to tear up the very old trees and replant with saplings, because young trees produce more fruit, although the old trees are very profitably exported to the French riviera to decorate country villas!

The olive harvest usually provides between two and three months of work each winter for people who normally do not earn wages (such as students and housewives) and for the seasonal workers who are home from the beach resorts. There is, also, increasing use of mechanical devices which shake the trees and suck up the olives like vacuum cleaners, and labour brought in from North Africa.

The pickers, according to their agreement with the farmer, can work by the day - *jornada* - or for a percentage of the value of the olives when weighed in at the mill. Another popular system is to agree on a flat price for picking an entire grove, called *ajustado*. The farmers vie for the fastest workers, and the rest usually find work in other parts of the region, such as the provinces of Cordoba and Jaen, where they live in sheds or old *cortijos*.

Like any other collective activity in Andalucia, the picking is done in a convivial atmosphere with a culture of its own. When the weather turns nasty in wintertime, at 900 meters above sea level, working from dawn to lunch (three o'clock) in the mud and wind can be arduous, and to make their lot more bearable the fun-loving Andalucians have developed a curious custom of chatting and joking, although it's less spontaneous than one might think. So much that some of the more loquacious and entertaining individuals are especially sought after when the teams are recruited, because they keep spirits up and make the work go faster.

The New and Old Cemeteries

Further to the right from our tower, but on the horizon, we see the long white wall and dark poplar trees of the town cemetery, the real one, where tombstones have become a thing of the past, largely superseded by the towering walls of multi-tiered crypts or *nichos*, each with its glass window and garland of artificial flowers. The advent of cheap building materials not only made it possible for people to indulge in their penchant for living one on top of the other, but also for being interred, or "inaired", that way.

This peculiar aversion to being buried down in the dank, worm-ridden earth stems for the Spanish fascination with mortality, so manifest in the works of artists such as Goya. As a friend of mine puts it, somehow the whole nasty thing seems less final when it ends up above ground. No fond sentimentalizing about eternal rest and endless natural cycles here, the horror of extinction is loudly voiced by all every time the awful word is mentioned. "*¡Qué bueno es poderlos escuchar!*", the villagers are wont to say, with a shudder, when the church bells toll for a funeral - "How good it is to be able to hear them!", which is a nice way of saying, thank God it isn't me. Another *dicho popular* which expresses their adamant refusal to find something good about the state of non-being is "*Los muertos al hoyo, y los vivos al bollo*", which translates loosely as "The dead, to their hole, and the living, to their bowl".

If you decide to drive rather than walk up the hill from the Plaza, you can park on a long platform of beaten earth officially called *El Cementerio Viejo*, the Old Cemetery, although in the Arrabal it's traditionally known as *El Panteón*, because the place went on being the town cemetery long after the church on the hill was abandoned in 1767. In the year 1901, for sanitary reasons (the villagers still drew their water from wells and there was danger of infiltration) the town graveyard was moved to its current site rather too far away on the eastern ridge, and everything covered in earth.

Not all the remains were dug up, though, because my friends in the Arrabal tell me that, when they were kids and played in the beaten soil, they came across "lots of bones"...

On the cliff face overlooking the place, the curious tunnels carved in the sandstone cliff are family vaults, the ancestors of the current *nichos*, and were reserved for the town's *personas principales*, or dignitaries and their families.

A last word, for now, on *el paso*, which is how death is delicately called here, "the crossing". The villagers were shocked when I told them that I myself hated cemeteries and wanted to be cremated, like a pagan! It reminded me of those first summers in Montefrio, when I casually mentioned to my singer friend Manolo that I had never been baptized. But the news hit him like a thunderbolt, even though in the Civil War he was "with" the anti-clerical Anarchists. He raised his arms and howled, as if he were intoning one of his *siguiriyas*, "Don't tell anyone that here, because they'll say you're the same thing as a horse!".

The other side of town, around El Convento

The eastern side of the town is distinguished by two landmarks, the royal silo called *El Pósito* and what is popularly known as *El Convento*. The *Pósito* was built in 1795 - at the same time as the round church, and as part of Carlos III's modernization program - to help stave off the famines which were common, as granary where the people could safely store their wheat; but it also acted as a rural credit bank which gave loans to the farmers against collateral in grain. There are very few of these *pósitos* left in Andalucia, and ours now functions as a handsomely appointed cultural center.

It is my theory that the *Pósito* was built on this site, on the rise overlooking the village from the east, rather than the seemingly logical area to the north and west of the town near the flatter land - and where the major crops are grown - because this was the closest point to the mills in the gorge below Parapanda Valley. It makes sense that the grain was taken directly from storage to be transformed there into flour and bread, rather than hauled across the town.

This would give some weight to the suggestion that the mills themselves were built by Carlos III at the end of the 18th century, although their importance for the granary would be the same had they been of Roman origin, as I feel sure.

"El Convento", or Church of San Antonio

Just up the hill from the *Pósito* stands the church of *San Antonio de Padua*, built in the baroque style in the mid-18th century. It is popularly known as *El Convento* because the adjacent building, recently restored, was once a Franciscan monastery, before being expropriated, like most of the Church´s huge landholdings, under the land reform of 1832, the tongue-twisting *Desamortización de Mendizábal*.

The charmingly naïve poem in my drawing of the church's impressive buttresses is by Lorca and says, "What's your street called? My street has no name. It's called the way it's called"…

31

After that the monastery was turned into a bakery, itself abandoned when the village bakers formed a cooperative in their shop near the Plaza. All of this has brought about a migration of names from one place to the other which is typical of these parts: the church is known as *El Convento* because of its proximity to the monastery, and the monastery is known as *La Máquina* because it once contained the machine which milled the town's flour.

[I should explain here that in Spanish convent does not exclusively mean a place for nuns nor does monastery only mean a place for monks. Rather, the words follow the original, Latin sense of a convent being a place where religious people come together or "convene" in communities which had a social as well as holy function, while a monastery is a where religious people live in solitude, on their own – "mono" – for the purpose of meditation and prayer. That is why most such establishments in Spain are called "conventos", whether there are men or women in them.]

From the belvedere in front of the church and the former convent-bakery we can see La Villa (cliff and church) and also the dome of the Iglesia de la Encarnación rising over the rooftops…

It is here, on the Plaza del Convento, that a lively neighbourhood fiesta is held every May 4th, known to all as *El Señor de los Pobres*, the "Christ of the Poor", with a procession in which ring-shaped rolls of bread, or *roscas*, are distributed to the crowd. A band plays and fireworks are launched into the night sky, with a crowd milling about, and everyone dances to the music of a well-amplified band. In the old days the religious procession with the hand-outs of bread formed the main attraction, but nowadays Andalucians are less concerned with salvation or starvation than having a good time, and the whole thing has become centered around the *baile* and the open-air bar.

The reason this curious holiday came about has, it seems, been forgotten by all except a few of the village's old-timers. One spring during the drought-ridden end of the 19th century, the people had prayed, to no avail, before all of the saints in the churches for rain to make the wheat grow. Then the priest of San Antonio de Padua had the idea of taking the figure of Christ in a holy procession around the town, on a cloudless afternoon – and in those days before tourism, blue skies meant hunger.

By the time the chanting crowd had returned to the church, thunder clouds were rolling overhead and after several days of continual rain the parched fields were quenched. The rolls given out symbolize the rescued wheat harvest, and the name of the holiday, *la Fiesta de la Caridad y Paciencia* (feast of charity and patience) clearly refers to our need to await the mercy of the Lord.

Until almost a century ago, there was an Easter week procession which led down from the Calvary Chapel on the hill and through the quarter called El Coro to San Antonio, but it was abandoned when the Church began cutting back on pageantry. Some of the crucifixes of the *Via Crucis* still stand along the road, so thickly coated in whitewash - applied by generations of those little women in black one sees embroidering on their tiny wicker chairs - that they seem to have become an organic part of the houses.

The last stretch before reaching the ruined chapel with its lichen-covered cross is a dirt and also rather dirty path which serves as a dump, but if you take the trouble to climb it you will be rewarded with a fairy-tale view of the town and castle, among the endless hills of olive groves.

El Coro

This drawing shows the girls of El Coro carrying water fresh in their *pipotes* from the fountain, and two old ladies in black sitting next to their ancient snow-white crucifix. The poem is, again, by Lorca, and speaks of an old woman in black "who thinks that the world is small and the heart immense".

Several hundred yards above the Convento the slope becomes steeper and, in the sunken alley on the right, you will see the first house which I restored, noticeable because of the magnificent grill over the window, of the sort which, late at night, young sweethearts desperately pressed their lips against to improvise a metallic sort of kiss, or, as was said, "eat iron"… The great wrought-iron *reja* once adorned one of the largest and most beautiful houses in the village, on the crossroads called *Las Esquinas de Jesus*, where I spent two summers during my student years. This enchanting "Moorish monastery", as I called it, was demolished to make way for a more symmetrical facsimile, but I was able to salvage the grill.

When I bought the Coro house as an office for my translation work, my first step was to have the relic straightened out and fix it to the façade - it took four of us just to lift it into place.

Casa del Coro,
Montefrío

The setting, while far humbler than the aristocratic old house near the plaza, makes the grill less likely to be troubled again, the neighbourhood not being at all attractive to modernizing property speculators.

When I first came to Montefrio, I would accompany my friend Manolo, the town butcher and one of Andalucia´s finest flamenco singers, up into *El Coro*, as the quarter is known ("the Choir", because it's high up, like the choir in a church). There, we would spend a musical hour with two gypsy brothers, Melchor and José, who were *cantaores* of considerable power and revered Manolo, musically at least.

Then, there was only a donkey path of beaten earth with boulders protruding everywhere, and lined by impoverished hovels covered with thatch roofs. Half-naked gypsy children played in the refuse while their mothers fanned charcoal burners to cook the daily stew. Some years, I learned on my return long afterwards, a fire destroyed most of the roofs and the Mayor had the houses tiled. Then, with Spain´s tourism boom, the inhabitants began to migrate north to work or peddle things, even sing and dance, in the resort areas of the Costa Brava and Mallorca. Thanks to the resulting influx of cash, later supplemented by the unemployment benefits which came into full force after Franco's death, the quarter was gradually upgraded to the point that it is now almost as respectable as the village's other working class quarters, with the special distinction that its inhabitants are gypsies.

From here up, therefore, you are in *terreno gitano*. The human atmosphere begins to get livelier and more "electric"; you may come across gaggles of young women with flashing dark eyes, shaking their lustrous manes of hair and displaying rows of gold rings on fingers tipped with blood-coloured nails. You may hear a burst of flamenco coming from some hidden stereo set or a housewife hanging out her laundry, chanting nasally as she holds up her husband's shirts to the sun. There is something festive and devil-may-care in the air, for you are, in fact, among a little tribe.

Unlike some other towns in the region, relations with the *gitanos* are relaxed, if not precisely affectionate, but fortunately we pale faces from afar are not thought of as being the garden variety of *payos* (non-gypsies), and all you have to do is smile and say *¡hola!* to get the same warm greeting in return.

Gypsies are a controversial subject and source of political embarrassment in Spain, so I should first confess that as a person I find most of them warm and responsive, as a writer I find almost all of them fascinating, as an artist I find quite a few of them beautiful, and as a lover of justice I feel that all of them have suffered enough. The gypsies may, for cultural rather than genetic reasons, have some of the defects which are ritually attributed to them by other Spaniards - largely as an excuse for excluding them from respectable walks of life - but it is my contention that the *payos* should now and then give them the benefit of the doubt, rather than keep doors closed firmly in their faces. I have spoken out on several occasions on their behalf, most loudly in protest against a local restaurant's mistreatment of several of my dearest friends. Although this incident occurred long ago – circa 1990 – and ended dramatically with the permanent departure of the proprietor, the fact that he was tacitly supported by many earned me some resentment among my fellow *Montefrieños*, who otherwise have always accepted me as a full-fledged villager. But they are indulgent – it's part of the admirable Catholic mentality, if not religion.

Here is a picture I drew for my postcard collection of the gypsies having fun in a street of *El Coro*, with the castle in the background. The poem is, again, by Federico García Lorca and says that anyone who ever visited "the city of the gypsies" can never forget it…

The only real street of the gypsy quarter is called Calle Coro y Visillo, "Coro and the Viewpoint". You can get to the famous viewpoint over the village by making your way along a path that leads to a pine grove, where there are several "semi-caves", as they are called, houses built against and into the rock.

The author rashly bought, or thought he bought, one of these caves, t thinking he would one day live there like a hermit. It turned out that the deed of purchase was useless because the caves had been banned from all human habitation due to the danger of reaching them along a flimsy walkway on the cliff face. So I consoled myself by drawing "my" cave, which you can see as you approach Montefrio along the old road coming from El Tocón.

I was sold it by a shepherd who kept his goats there, quaintly known as El Tipo, and he told me its strange and tragic story. The cave is known to the old-timers as la *cueva de las gazapillas*, which literally means "the cave of the little female rabbits". It was the home of a man nicknamed El Gazapo, the little rabbit, and he lived there with his wife, two daughters and small son, earning his keep as a truck-driver's assistant. When the Civil War broke out he went away and never returned, leaving his family destitute in a time of great hardship...

The fate of the people of Andalucia was particularly cruel during the war, because most of them supported the Republican forces, and the villagers, left to their own devices, were reduced to living on roots and leaves, during the conflict and for years afterwards. The old-timers tell of the outbreaks of *sarna* - mange - which plagued them, with everyone scratching their skin, due to the appalling conditions and malnutrition. Alas, war is much more than just men shooting bullets at one another, if you're caught in the middle of it.

Montefrio, like the rest of Granada Province, was taken over by Franco's troops during the first months of fighting and a garrison was placed at the bridge to control the entrance to the village, just below the cliffs. Since the soldiers had food, a crowd of women and barefoot children appeared silently around the mess tent when the cook ladled the stew into the tin plates. Since we've all seen photographs of the time, we can imagine the threadbare black dresses, the thin legs and the dust of the army lorries which rolled in and out of the town.

The two now fatherless sisters, then in their teens, came down from their cave too, and before long the soldiers were trysting with them in the bushes under the bridge. As the war progressed, the girls became plump and, being no longer in immediate need of food, began charging for their services, and when dusk fell the soldiers would climb the hill to line up in front of the cave. It became a well-organized brothel, one of several which were to be found in the town during those threadbare times. When a woman had nothing to feed her children, the last resort was to *alquilar el humero* - "rent out her chimney", as mothers will do everywhere.

There is (at least there was when I visited the cave) a front room and a bedroom in the back. As El Tipo told it to me, the girls, by this time known as *las gazapillas* - the nickname they inherited, in the feminine and diminutive form, from their departed Dad - took their customers through the parlour, where the mother and boy were sitting around the oil lamp. The family was so businesslike that when the girls were away "working" in Granada, the mother took over for them, rather than lose the clientele. The cave was always spanking clean, beautifully whitewashed and with pots of geraniums hanging gaily around the door - the *gazapillas* ran a tight ship. When I asked the old man if he too had patronized them (although that wasn't the word I used) he smiled nostalgically and croaked, "We all did".

Then the war ended and the soldiers went away. The women began to serve the local market, and when the village men went on a binge they would end up knocking on their door, late at night. Until one day the village women's fuse burned out and a gang of them marched up to the cave, waving saucepans and crying "Get out of here, you *marranas* - pigs!". The *gazapillas* packed up and moved to Granada, and the abandoned cave was used as a shelter by tramps – *indigentes* -. who drifted through the village, until El Tipo took it over for his goats.

LAS PEÑAS DE LOS GITANOS

Montefrio's prehistóric archaeological site

The remains of Montefrio's Iberian settlement have been known to archaeologists for almost as long as interest in unwritten history has existed. The discipline was "invented" in the Renaissance because scholars wanted to unearth Greek and Roman monuments to use as architectural models in the classical revival, but it was not until the 19th century that scholars first became interested in all ancient things, whether they belonged to the times before the Greeks and Romans or after them, simply because they tell us about what we once were, in a spirit of unbiased curiosity. Desire for knowledge for its own sake had come of age.

The new movement was born with the Scottish creation of the "Society of Antiquarians", and soon touched imaginations as far away as in Spain. Granada's first *anticuario* was one Don Manuel de Góngora, a professor of history, and in the summer of 1868 this lonely pioneer led an expedition through the wilderness of Andalucia in search of prehistoric remains, which he described in a small book handsomely illustrated with etchings called *Antigüedades de Andalucía*. The peasants of Montefrio led him up from the plain through the Gorge of the Mills to a forbidding range of cliffs and meadows, where hundreds of curious slabs of stone, forming boxlike constructions, jutted out of the earth.

Góngora wrote that not only was that natural citadel rich in remains, but that the path leading to it from Montefrio was "strewn with tombs on either side". Since then, bulldozers and explosives have enabled the farmers to remove these obstructions from their fields, so that only those among the cliffs, where the terrain is too rough for farming, have survived.

Our corner of Spain is, first and foremost, a sprawling open-air history book whose successive chapters can be "read" by the curious traveller, in a blessed landscape of oak forests, limestone cliffs and hidden valleys, stony mountains and rolling olive groves. Montefrio may have no single monument of great importance in itself – there are better preserved Moorish forts, more elegant Renaissance churches, larger and more complex prehistoric tombs in other parts of Andalucia – but it is unrivalled for the continuity and harmony of the ensemble, virtually unspoiled by modern progress.

The site, which towers above the road from Montefrio to Puerto Lope, some 5 kilometers east of the town, was the main center of population in the region for over 5,000 years. It contains the remains, many inaccessible or in shambles, of several hundred dolmens – the "stone tables" of the ancient Britons, better described as megalithic tombs – as well as a Roman fort and an early medieval village. Several archaeological excavations have been made since Gongora's discovery, but they have barely scratched the surface of the remains believed to exist, both buried in the ground and hidden in the region's caves. In Spain, there are many antiquities, but not enough money to salvage them.

The name of the place itself tells us something about its more recent history: the Cliffs of the Gypsies, so called because, until the end of the 18th century, Spain's gypsies, who roamed the country working as weavers, tinkers, musicians and fortune-tellers, as well as begging and stealing, were not allowed to live within several miles of the nearest town. Our gypsies camped here among the cliffs and meadows, although there no traces of their presence remain.

This maze-like, multi-levelled region, which stretches over several miles, resembles a great gash thrown up among the rolling hills of olive groves. Years ago, in my first book, I drew this simple map to help the traveller find a few of the many points of interest.

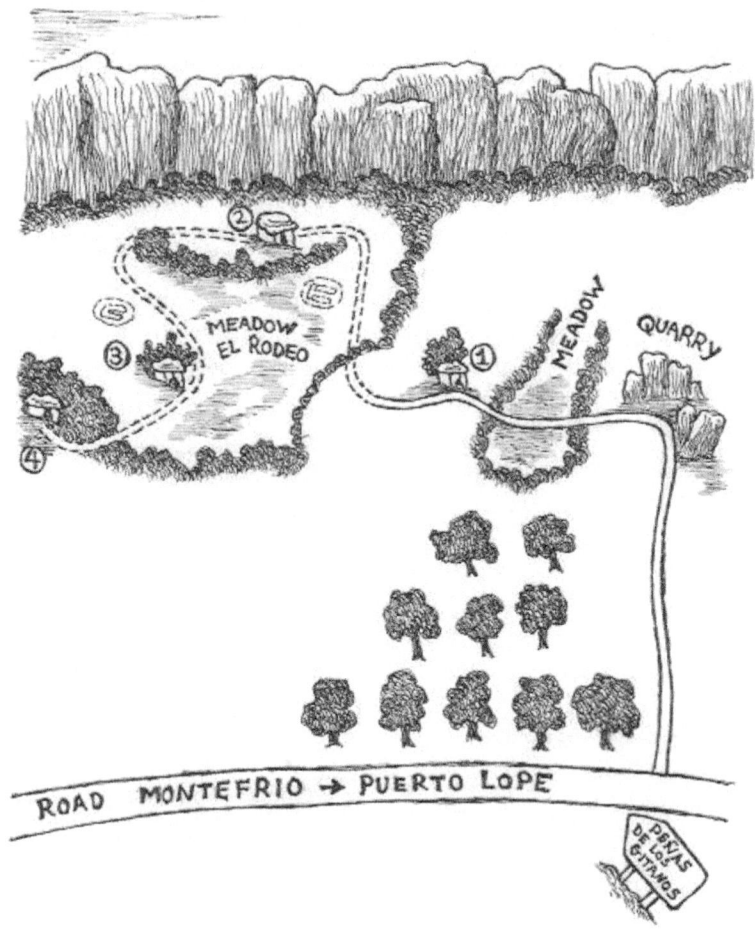

El Rodeo and its Dolmens

This is the best-known part of the site, because of the prehistoric tombs which stand on the large meadow known as *El Rodeo*, at the foot of a mighty wall of cliffs. The dirt road leading there runs through an abandoned quarry at the foot of the cliffs and, several hundred yards on, crosses a small meadow, ending in a round-about at the second, much larger meadow, El Rodeo (pronounced ro-DAY-o). In the short stretch between the two meadows, on the right-hand side of the road, stands a finely built dolmen, the covering slab of which has been thrown to one side by the almond tree growing in its midst. These tombs are composed of a mortuary chamber in which hundreds of bodies were buried, with access through a long, narrow corridor and small door carved in the front slab. The front slab is usually composed of two stones fitted together with a notch in each forming a door, but in this dolmen the aperture was gouged out of a single piece, making it especially impressive. I often wonder why no one has taken the trouble to root out the invading almond tree and put the stones back in their places, because this is one of the most beautiful examples we have.

On the floor of the vast meadow, spectacularly framed among cliffs and stony mountains, we see a number of rectangular cuts in the reddish soil, which the archaeologists made to reveal other similar tombs. Most of them have lost their covering slabs, but there are three dolmens on and around the meadow which are intact, and the best known, and most photographed, of them all stands on a low rise overlooking the meadow itself. From the roundabout, walk towards the cliffs on the right, skirting around the foot of the rise until you find a rough path leading up to the plateau.

There are two tombs here, and the first one is in perfect condition, only lacking one of the stones which form the entrance corridor. The tomb just beyond it, however, is in total ruin, its massive slabs cast on all sides. There was a spate of grave-plundering in the 1950's, after several well-publicized caches of treasure were found by demolition workers in houses of Granada's old Moorish quarter, the Albaicin, apparently hidden there by the original occupants when they were expelled from Spain in the 16th century. Many of the rich Moors preferred to leave their wealth behind, in the widely prevalent belief that they would one day be allowed to return, rather than risk having it confiscated by the Christians as they left the country, or by their fellow Moors when they reached the other shore of the Mediterranean. Since the local people believed, and many still believe, that all ancient remains are the work of *los moros*, upon hearing about the treasures they set about tearing apart all of the tombs which had not been previously plundered by the Romans, and when the stones were too heavy to move they blew them up with dynamite, something the Romans didn't have, even though all they found were bones, flints and clay pots.

I first came to Montefrio not long after the treasure-hunting craze, and one summer evening a farmer came to our house in the village saying that his wife had had a dream about a tomb in the Peñas which was full of gold and jewels, and that if my companion and I could bring from Germany a machine he had heard about capable of detecting such materials, he would be willing to share the treasure with us!

The other two dolmens lie across the meadow, to the south, hidden by a clump of oak trees and somewhat smaller and rougher than the tomb on the rise. The third intact dolmen which can be easily visited is inside the thicket of oak trees which stands on the rim of the meadow just beyond, and is different from the others because it is more deeply imbedded in the surface, and because its "door" is composed of two rectangular slabs set several feet apart to form the door, without the usual notches.

The people of the prehistoric settlement grazed their sheep and buried their dead down on the meadow, but they lived in a safe place high up on the cliffs, the *Poblado de los Castillejos*, to the west. Leaving the village on the road to Puerto Lope and Granada, turn left after the bridge over the ravine, taking the dirt road up the hill to the huge old farmhouse called El Cortijo del Castillón. Continue on foot along the very rough road which branches off to the right, between the farmhouse and the Castillón Hill, heading east towards the cliffs.

The Roman Fort and El Poblado

The outcropping of rock which rises before us is the site of the Roman fortress, but before climbing to the top we should examine the curious cave at its foot. It would seem to be part of the ancient military outpost because its mouth is partly sealed with a wall of large, symmetrically carved stones which may have once framed a door. It seems that the Romans used the cave, spacious and high inside, as a storage area for the fort.

On the plateau above the cave are several rows of massive, squared stones which are all that is left of the fortress. Some of the stones have small notches cut in the upper edge, facing one another from stone to stone to form a butterfly-shaped cavity, into which molten lead was poured to clamp the stones firmly together.

The view from the plateau sweeps across the fertile valley below. It may be that the Romans chose this place because it allowed them to control the comings and goings through the Gorge of the Mills, where they had built the series of flour mills which would have been the driving force of the region's economy.

Further on are the excavated remains of the Roman "Poblado" or settlement, with a small grid of walls. The far end of the small plateau is occupied by the corrugated iron hangar which was erected by the archaeologists to protect their most recent excavation. There is an opening in the far side which enables us to look in.

What we see appears, to the untrained eye, to be nothing but a large, square hole. Thousands of years ago, the ground level was at the bottom of the excavation, 7 meters down, and it effectively rose with the passing of time, to the level on which we are standing. When the first settlers arrived, the surface of the plateau was shaped like a deep groove or canyon between two natural walls of stone, and the tribe chose this slot between the rocks to build their thatch-and-wattle huts to be protected from rain and storm. As the huts crumbled and were replaced, other huts were built on top of their remains, so that the ground level imperceptibly rose – at the rate, I calculate, of 1.5 meters every thousand years – until it had effectively emerged from its snub corridor. The silt and detritus left by the village filled the slot completely, forming the smooth surface which the plateau has today.

Seen from inside the hangar, the hole seems more meaningful. The walls provide us with a cross-section of the village's many layers, showing how the villagers stored their grain in clearly silhouetted round-bottomed grain silos. These were small pits dug in the earth and lined with mud which hardened, and then they were then filled with grain and covered, as protection against rats and insects. The horizontal white strips are the ashes left by the cooking fires.

A huge slab of stratified rock lies on the floor of the pit, which is believed to have been attached to the upper part of the southern wall, forming a sort of roof overhanging the narrow canyon. Ulises, a young archaeologist I found there at work one day, and whom I shall henceforth call by the English translation of his name, explained to me that he at first thought it could have been struck by a lightning bolt and fallen onto the village at its early beginnings, but the fact that it lies on the rock bottom, rather than on the accumulation of silt left by the village, made him decide that it fell before the arrival of the first inhabitants, who simply built their huts around, and eventually on top of it.

On one of my many visits to the site he showed me a tear-shaped amber bead he had discovered, pierced with a tiny hole. We imagined it had hung from a necklace some Iberian lass had lost in the alleys of her village, three or four thousand years ago...

[Later I went to see his progress on the shore of a manmade lake south of Granada. Because of a long drought, the water level fell so low that a whole strand which had been covered since Franco built the dam appeared, with on it, as if they were bathers taking the sun, some twenty stone coffins of the same sort he found in Montefrio. Ulysses had been hired to empty them one by one, which filled his jeep for several days with skulls, femurs, earthenware pots and the usual bone earrings and necklaces...]

After attentively examining the ruins of the past, we can pay tribute to the freshness of the present, at least in Andalucia, by walking to the end of the plateau and gazing out at the sublime perspective of the hills and valleys lying between Montefrio and Granada. Before us is a topsy-turvy mosaic of olive groves, oak forests and naked peaks, dotted with farmhouses shining in the sun "like doves", as the Andalucian women proudly say, when they have finished whitewashing their homes.

A path plunges down through a narrow crack in the rocks, leading to a gaping cavern which was the original entrance to the village. To return to the farmhouse, we double back up this path a few steps and head down through the meadow which lies behind the plateau.

EL CERRO DEL CASTILLÓN
the medieval citadel

This time, we will set out from the *Cortijo del Castillón* towards the south, to visit what is perhaps the most fascinating, and least known, of Montefrio's ancient sites. The hill which we are going to explore resembles – to me who lived in full view of it for ten years - an island covered in oak trees, thrown up among the mass of cliffs like a humpbacked whale. For some six centuries, the second half of which under Moorish domination, it was the site of a village inhabited by the descendants of the Spaniards of antiquity, of mixed Iberian and Roman descent. They were called Mozarabic – "like Arabs" - because they had assimilated the culture and language of the Arabs but not the religion. The Cerro del Castillón was, therefore, a recalcitrant Christian enclave during the Islamic period, constantly harassed and finally engulfed by the invaders.

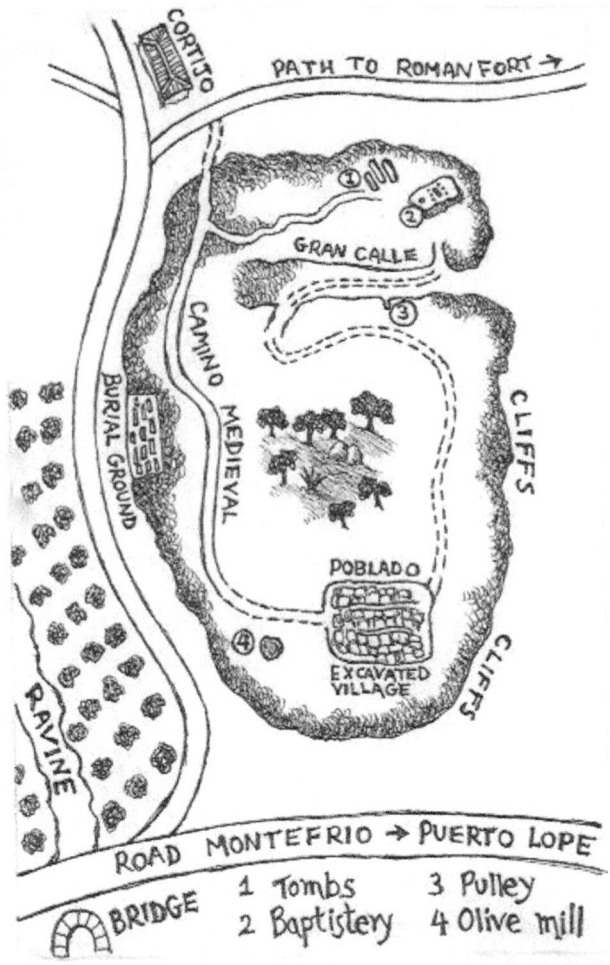

CORTIJO

PATH TO ROMAN FORT →

GRAN CALLE

① ☐ ②
③

CAMINO MEDIEVAL

BURIAL GROUND

CLIFFS

POBLADO
④
EXCAVATED VILLAGE

CLIFFS

RAVINE

ROAD MONTEFRIO → PUERTO LOPE

BRIDGE

1 Tombs
2 Baptistery
3 Pulley
4 Olive mill

Such pockets of open resistance to Islam were common in very remote places like Montefrio, as reported by Ibn Hawqal, the 10th century Mesopotamian geographer and chronicler. He wrote thus of the rural *mozárabe* communities in Muslim Spain: "In *al-Andalus* there are great domains on which toil thousands of wretched and ignorant peasants of European stock who stubbornly cling to their Christian faith. Sometimes they rebel against their Arab lord and flee to a hilltop which they set about fortifying. It can be very difficult to bring them back and punish them because they are proud and defiant, often making it necessary to slay them to the last man, which can be long and arduous."

This expressive illustration from a medieval manuscript, depicting the old Christians of Moorish Spain, helps us imagine those beleaguered early *Montefrieños* who built their crudely carved citadel on the Cerro del Castillón.

Historians, however, believe that the hill was used as a refuge even before the arrival of the Moors in 711. It may be assumed that, immediately after the fall of the Empire, and under the rule of the triumphant Visigoths, the community continued to live between the protection of the cliffs and the fertile plain below. Very little must have changed during two long centuries – it is even possible that none of the warlike Visigoths ever visited Montefrio, since the new masters were few in number and lived largely in the towns, where their princes and bishops were forever vying with one another for power.

But in the 6th century, the far south of Spain was invaded by the Byzantines, who wanted to win back the Empire created by their Roman ancestors. They moved into the western Mediterranean, taking southern Italy, Carthage, and the southern shore of the peninsula, with the ultimate aim of controlling the Straits of Gibraltar, in order to bring back the old Mare Nostrum.

The Byzantines gave up their over-ambitious project in the following century, but before they withdrew from Spain they had to fight off the attacks of the Visigoths. Thus, they turned Montefrio's farmlands into a battle zone, since the invaders occupied the plain of Granada up to the foot of the Sierra de Parapanda. It was then that the peasants of the valley took refuge on the heights of the *Cerro del Castillón*, perhaps preferring it to the old acropolis of *Los Castillejos* because, being shaped like an isolated hump, it was easier to defend. And when the Moors arrived, sixty years after the departure of the Byzantines, the inhabitants would have found no good reason to come down from their refuge.

Mozarabic uprisings against the Caliphate

In spite of what is often claimed, the Christians as well as the Jews did not have a happy life in Muslim society. At the beginning, when the Moors' position – as a minority in a hostile country where people were either Pagans, Christians or a mixture of both – was still weak, they were more benign and tolerant. But under the great Caliphate of Cordoba, in the 10th century, the Moors finally succeeded in federating their various clans or *taifas* which had been fighting constantly against one another since the invasion of 711. The huge power which this put in the Cordovans' hands enabled them to strike out against the dreaded Christians of the realm, who had openly rebelled against the Caliph.

The inhabitants of enclaves such as the Castillón – and, on a far larger scale, the citadel of Bobastro near Malaga, whose basilica carved into the rock is still visible - were forced to leave their perches and roosts and go down to live on the lowlands, where it would be easier to govern, and to tax them. The Moorish fiscal system was severe even by medieval standards, requiring Christians to pay a special tax or *yizya* just in order to practice their faith.

One thing is certain about their fate in Montefrio: the remains found on the hill show that it was abandoned at this period. It was then that the Caliph's soldiers established a military post there, presumably to watch over the natives. The site they chose was several miles west of the cliffs, on and around the great promontory which ever since has been called Montefrio.

The Necropolis, or burial ground

On the Castillón Hill, as in the prehistoric settlement above El Rodeo, the people lived on high and buried their dead below. The small part of their necropolis, excavated in the winter of 1980-81, lies on the right hand side of the road leading up from the highway to the farmhouse.

Some 100 tombs, really coffins made of slabs of stone, have been laid bare. Although the people were Christians, many pagan beliefs and practices survived, such as the burial of the dead with their earthly possessions. Accordingly, the men had a small earthenware jug full of olive oil placed next to their heads, and the women were buried wearing a pair of bronze hoop earrings.

As many as three or four skeletons were found in some of them, suggesting that the villagers were unable to build enough graves for their dead and had to re-use old tombs, placing the bones of the previous occupant at the foot of the grave and the skull on one side at the head, to make way for a new body. This "crowding" could be explained both by the fact that the village grew suddenly in size, receiving refugees from other places, and, also, that the people were too busy fighting off the Moors to expand their cemetery.

[It should be made clear that the official description of the burial ground as being "Visigothic" – *visigodo* – simply means that it dates from the time when Spain was ruled by the Visigoths. Few of the real Visigoths left the major cities, and it may even be true that not a single one of them ever wandered as far into the boondocks as the confines of Montefrio.]

The Medieval Road

The road of access to the citadel skirts around the west side of the hill and was clearly intended for the use of carts, possibly drawn by oxen. There was no source of water on the hill, and the inhabitants would have had to carry it up in jugs from the spring in the valley to the west of the hill, La Fuente del Castillón.

Following my map, we cross the meadow at the foot of the hill and enter the forest of oak trees by what at first is only a path but, as soon as it begins to climb upwards, begins to belie its ancient origins. By carving into the bedrock and heaping boulders along the outer side of the road, a cradle-shaped groove was formed which was then filled with rubble to form a smooth surface. The small stones which litter the road are what remains of the original pavement, and 1,500 years of erosion have taken care of the rest.

The Military Gate

Once we reach the plateau, the traces of the road disappear in the midst of a small meadow, but the large vertical slab of rock in its center, which at first glance resembles a *menhir* or "standing stone", is, I believe, the remains of the military gate which defended the citadel. By looking closely at the surface to its west, we can see the line of half-buried stones which runs towards the edge of the cliff. The wall seems to have closed off the entrance to the road between this point and the ridge on the east, and the great stone formed one side of the gate, which could have been barricaded with timbers in time of danger.

The Cliff Road

We make our way along the path, among stones and bushes, until we come to the most impressive stretch of all, the cliff road. Here, the road had to be cut into the steep face of the cliff, on one side, and built out onto a retaining wall on the other to give it the necessary breadth. If the angle of the light is favourable, you can see the scratches which the cartwheels made in the corner of the cliff and the road.

It is easy to imagine the men pushing and whipping their beasts of burden as the cart, heavily laden with jugs of water, slithered along the narrow road, in constant danger of sliding over the edge. The archaeologists tell me that this part of the road, being exposed to the view from below, was protected from the arrows of the marauding enemies by a stockade, because there are notches carved in the cliff above, to secure the timbers.

The excavated village

We continue to skirt around the west side of the plateau, following the path down through the oak trees until we come to the grid of village houses which was excavated in 1981, known as *el poblado*, at the southernmost tip of the plateau.

The maize-like skeleton of stones on the brink of the plateau, sparsely framed in small, dark-leafed oak trees, is tilted face to face with the mountain and the valley, forming a great, fertile funnel which in turn plunges into the cleft between the Sierra de Parapanda and the

Sierra del Tocón. This opening in the range - the Gorge of the Mills – provides us with a wedge-shaped window looking down on the plain of Granada. And beyond the undulating expanse of the Vega rises yet another range of mountains, the Sierra de Almuñécar, standing like a hazy screen between us and the Mediterranean, whose brilliance is mirrored up behind the peaks.

We know from the shards excavated that the roofs of the houses were tiled and at least one of them had a crude mosaic floor, probably imitating one the owner had seen in the Roman "villas" of the valley below, or in the Roman Granada.

This part of the village was crossed from east to west by two clearly visible parallel streets, and the curious double walls between several of the houses, running from north to south (downhill) were gutters for rain and sewage water. The Castillón Citadel is a remote outpost of late Roman civilization, whose people were a mixture of native Iberians and Romans, spoke a form of Latin and practiced a mixture of Christianity and paganism, but who by tradition were and considered themselves to be sons of Rome. We know, from the finds which have been made, that their way of living and working was Roman, with their own manufacture of pottery, cloth, ironwork and, as we will now see, olive oil...

The Olive Oil Mill

This, however, means going back a stone's throw on our steps, if we have followed the Medieval Road as shown on my map. But it makes more sense to speak of the mill after the description of the village, of which it was surely an essential part…

At the lower end of the slope, where we turn east towards the ruins, stands a curious stone which was nothing less than our community's olive oil mill (the Romans introduced olive trees and the use of oil in the 2nd century).

It seemed amazing to me, in spite of the clearly "worked" appearance of this heart-shaped stone, several meters in length and standing a good meter high, that the University archaeologists made no mention of it in their handsomely-produced publication, which is strictly devoted to the results of their excavations. Like the ostrich which buries its head in the sand, it would seem that nothing was of interest to them if it was not underground!

My own attention was called to the existence of this impressive object, probably one of the oldest olive oil mills in Spain, by Juan, the local shepherd, who had no doubt what it was and showed me how, were it not for the effects of so many centuries of erosion, it could be used to make oil today.

A lip has been cut around the edge of the flattened surface to prevent the precious liquid from escaping, giving the stone the form of a platter or tray. In the center a small hole has been bored into the surface to anchor the grinding stone which was dragged around over the olives. The angle of the rock, which may have been accentuated by the oak tree growing out from underneath it, caused the oil to flow down through the opening or "spout" cut into the lower end of the rim.

At first, I wondered how they prevented the oil from dripping down the side of the stone and being lost in the earth, but when I walked around and parted the bushes I saw that there is a mouth-shaped incision just below the spout, in which a rounded tile could be fitted to draw the oil off for collection in a jug.

Perhaps the only thing which is more astonishing than the object itself is the fact that until the present day the only person who has noticed and written about it is me!

The Fort

After visiting the village, we make our way up the eastern side of the plateau, along the edge of the towering cliff which overlooks Las Peñas. There are many convenient stones to sit on, so that we can catch our breath as we gaze over, or down on, the magnificent landscape. If you keep a careful eye on the ground, difficult as this may seem when surrounded with such scenery, you will see many straight rows of semi-buried stones, testifying to the fact that the entire citadel was covered in houses. The squarish holes cut in the stone, several feet wide, were watering holes for animals or, perhaps, silos for storing grain. Other smaller round holes were used as sockets for the joists of wooden houses.

We come out onto the smooth summit of the hill. The only object which catches our eye, as we begin to cross the meadow, is a smaller and more primitive olive oil mill, resembling a long basin half-imbedded in the ground, with a curious hole bored in the side. The olives (as well, certainly, as grains of cereal) were crushed by hand with stones, and the accumulated liquid dripped through this spout into a receptacle.

The knoll ends abruptly in a precipice overlooking an inner canyon, which cuts across the entire hill from east to west like a corridor. This is the highest part of the promontory, and its stony crown bears a single, minute trace which makes it clear that this was once the fortress of the community, the place where the inhabitants took refuge when under attack.

On my map it is designated as The Pulley. At the very edge of the precipice, a narrow groove – about 4 inches in width, and 6 deep – has been cut, in a curved shape which leaves no doubt that it was used to haul things up from below. It is my belief that the early inhabitants of the hill, who lived not at the southernmost point which we have visited, but in the corridor below, used this pulley to haul up baskets of supplies when the citadel was being besieged. It is easy to imagine ten or twenty men pulling together on a rope greased with animal fat, while their comrades kept the Moors at bay.

The "Great Street" – La Gran Calle

If you're nimble enough, you can find your way down into the ravine, known by historians as La Gran Calle, by walking west along the edge of the cliff and climbing down a "staircase" along the rocks.

Pushing aside the undergrowth, we step out onto the floor of a long groove in the rock, surrounded on both sides some 50 feet high, so that all we can see above them is a long strip of sky. This natural enclosure was once crowded with huts, and the rubble which litters the ground is what remains of the materials of which they were made.

As we walk east through the ravine, we can see on our left a number of hollows carved out of the cliff. These are the remains of rupestrian (rock) dwellings, or semi-caves, which were covered with branches and leaves and equipped with stairs and niches used as hearths and shelves. On our right, there is a ramp carved in the cliff face, leading up to the fort. Further on, you can make out the "pulley" etched against the sky, and, 20 yards ahead, a number of notches for climbing up the rock face in a hurry. Try and you'll see that it works perfectly, up to the part of the rock which has been split and covered by invading vegetation. This was an "emergency escape" ladder, making it possible to scramble up into the fort when danger threatened.

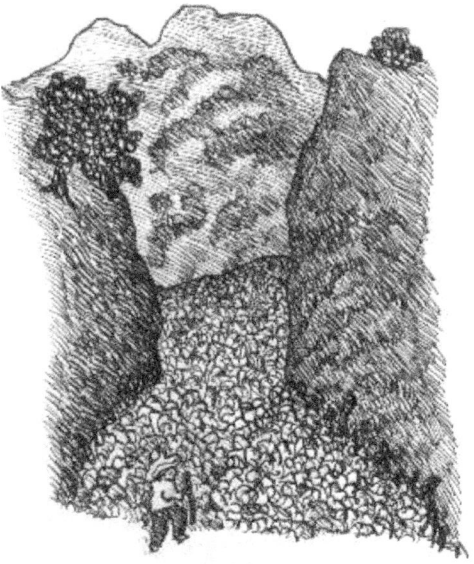

We leave the Gran Calle by a gap in the opposite side of the ravine, and climb several steps up onto the northernmost part of the plateau, the place which I call the "church" because of the nature of its rock carvings. Near the electrical pylon are three tombs cut into the stone, which have long since lost the lids which fitted into the surrounding notches. And several steps toward the west, in the direction of the great cliffs of Las Peñas across the valley, we discover what are for me, and for many of my friends, the most intriguing and evocative remains of all of Montefrio's treasures.

The "child of the Castillón"

The baptistery means much to me, so I am first going to tell the story of my friendship with the shepherd who helped me find it.

One day I stopped at the Castillón farmhouse to buy some eggs from Juan's wife Maria. The old man invited me in to sit with him by the fire, where he was drying his boots, and showed me a small clay jug with a broken handle which, he said, a tractor had thrown up, along with parts of a skeleton, in the field above his house, while digging holes to plant olive saplings. In his opinion, the jug was *cosa de los moros* – made by the Moors – and probably worthless. At that time I was raising ducks at my *cortijo* down the path, one of which was a male which Juan said he wanted. The deal was struck immediately: a bird weighing two kilos for a funereal urn from the Dark Ages.

I then visited the site of the discovery, where I saw how the *tractorista* had dug his hole in the very middle of the long, flat stones which form the same tombs which have been excavated on the Castillón Hill. Juan's son had already planted the sapling, still in its black plastic bag, and when I reproachfully asked him, "Why didn't you dig the hole a little to one side, so as to spare the tomb?", he replied that the olive trees were always planted in perfectly symmetrical rows and at the same distance from one another, and that the spot for that tree was there. Keeping my indignation, once more, to myself, I gathered up the bones which had been scattered everywhere, and kept the scraps of skull, jaw, femurs and teeth in a cupboard, along with the small urn.

Now that Juan realizes how much his neighbour is interested in the subject, he never fails to show me his discoveries in the surrounding woods, which he roams every afternoon with his flock of goats. In turn, I faithfully translate for him the letters he receives each year from the Pensions Department of the city of Auch in southwestern France, where he worked as a farmhand during his youth. In order to continue collecting his tiny French pension, our Town Hall must certify that he is still alive, since the descendants of retired immigrant workers do not always give notice of their passing.

[To think that today I'm doing the same thing for myself but in reverse – collecting a yearly *certificat de vie* from the *Mairie* of Nice to mail to the Pensions Department in Granada, to be paid my old age pension for the twenty years I worked in Spain as a translator!]

Juan showed me the olive oil mill, several dolmens in the ravine between the Castillón and Las Peñas, and the baptistery. At about the same time as his priceless gift I was walking on the hill with two students from Oxford University who were staying in one of my houses, when I met him grazing his goats near the tombs, at the foot of the high-tension pylon which his son-in-law – the owner of the farm – installed when he electrified the farm. "There's *un niño* carved in the rock over there", the old man said gruffly. "Must be another invention of those damned *moros*".

The next day I was there with my two guests, equipped with a scrubbing brush and a few litters of water from the spring below, to remove the moss and wash the stone clean, so that we could see what we had. As the reader may have guessed, I have been in love with the thing ever since.

First of all, we should consider the natural base, a large stone about a meter high which could easily have been used as an altar. Around the carving which my friend called *el niño* there are 15 symmetrical holes, about 5 inches in width and 8 in depth, forming a sort of wreath around the child, which could have been filled with oil to make lamps. Outside this magical circle are two other, much larger holes, bored at an angle, one to the west and another behind the feet of the child, although there is certainly a third one to the east, where a bush has taken root. Three tree trunks could have been inserted in these holes, tied together at the tops like a wigwam and covered with branches to form a chapel of boughs. Allowing for fifteen centuries of erosion, these holes are perfectly bored, as if an iron bit had been used.

The child is also perfectly chiselled in the stone in the tapered shape of a mummy, with a small, symbolic "head" and squared "feet". When we filled it with water, the reflection of the sky on the surface made this shape even more unmistakable. One of the women with me was a student of theology and explained that the early Christians baptized by immersion rather than sprinkling. We imagined a ceremony held at dawn, with the parents standing in front of the stone, and the priest kneeling on top of it before the font, lowering the shivering baby into the cold water, brought up from the same spring as ours, but in an earthenware jug...

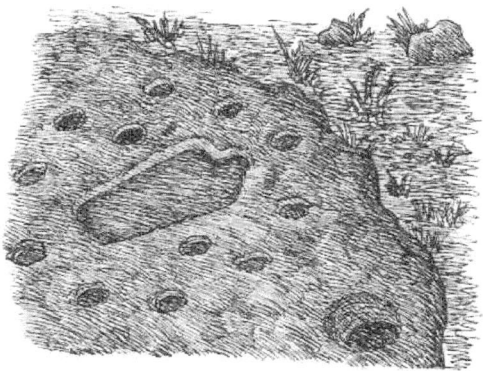

An unresolved mystery

The Archaeological Museum of Madrid possesses, among its many medieval exhibits, a child's sarcophagus of soft, porous stone from the 13th century, found in northern Spain, which has a detail strikingly in common with our font: the small, symbolic head, giving it the same mummy-like appearance. Otherwise, our "child" is in every way as valuable as the one in the museum: it is many centuries older, because we know that the hill was abandoned at the turn of the millennium; it is surrounded with the mysterious array of holes; it is in far better condition because the granite is harder, and, above all, it is too shallow and exposed to be a sarcophagus, which means that it can only be a baptistery, and therefore more precious.

Later, when I was doing the research for my book, I organized an official visit to the hill, with the Mayor of the village, several of our school teachers, and the Chief Archaeologist of the University of Granada who, as a student, took part in the excavation of 1980-81. She seemed quite embarrassed to have to admit that she had never noticed either the olive oil mill nor the baptistery, and when I showed her the latter, she stared at it for a long time and only muttered, "I have never seen anything like it", declining any further comment. Which means, if it really is a baptismal font, that *el niño del Castillón* must be the only known example of a rupestrian baptistery made during the Moorish period. The church itself would appear to have been on the flat land nearby, which is in accordance with the early Christian practice of placing the baptistery outside of the temple itself. With so many pagans converting to the new faith, entrance to the church was restricted to those who had already been christened, which meant that baptisms had to be performed outside, near the front door.

Sadly, the Professor never returned to the site accompanied with experts, as she promised the Mayor and me. Down in the dusty rooms of the *Facultad*, the professors and students of archaeology, almost all of them the daughters of distinguished, or at least well-off families – beginning with Doña Conchita herself - are too busy labelling the cabinets full of pottery found on their expeditions in the region. There is no definition which fits the baptistery of Montefrio in their manuals, and nothing similar to it in their collections, and therefore it does not exist.

My academic friends have even maliciously suggested that the Professor would be reluctant to publicize objects which she herself failed to notice during an entire winter of visiting the place every day. To make her even more reluctant to risk her good name, they had been discovered, not only by a simple shepherd like Juan, but by a writer who would make noise if she were to take the credit for herself.

This said, I invite lovers of history, art and science everywhere to help me unveil the mystery of this haunting message from the past, scratched over 1,000 years ago in the stone of an Andalucian hilltop.

Here is a photograph I had taken of the strange carvings, with my forearm for the scale and the child-shaped cavity half-filled with water. The drawing is more graphic, but forcibly less realistic.

Rogelio, our own saint

We have little to go on except archaeology to trace the history of the region around Montefrio because very few documents remain from before the Christian reconquest and very little after that either. It's the fate of a farming village where the landholders – the only people who could have left written information – usually lived in the cities and only came here to claim their due from the peasants. The same held for the "Ibero-Romans", the inhabitants of the old Roman colony Hispania, and the Moors who replaced them.

In spite of the darkness of the centuries, however, one name linked to the region and the aforementioned period of strife has come down to us, that of Rogelio. This austere monk was from the neighbouring village of Illora (of which he is now the patron saint) and lived in the 9th century. As a Christian in Islamic territory he was known in Arabic as *mozarab* – which euphemistically meant "an Arabized Christian". Most of the old Christians either emigrated north to flee the Muslims or stayed on and gradually joined them – it was common to pragmatically convert, just to avoid being a second-class subject and having to pay the punitive poll tax. Rogelio and a small band of other brave souls, though, clung to the faith of their already distant ancestors, and to practice it in peace went to live in a crude monastery they built nearby, on the flanks of the Sierra de Parapanada.

Rogelio – then called *Rogellus*, since Spaniards still spoke Latin, or a version thereof - enters history after the year 850, when the "mozarabs" of Cordoba revolted against the increasingly domineering Mohammedans. News of this inspired Rogelio and several of his companions to journey to the Moorish capital to share the sufferings of their bretheren. Such a mission – and provocation – could only end in the holy martyrdom which Rogelio and his friends sought.

In Cordoba, they entered the Great Mosque on Friday – the Muslim holy day - disguised as Moors. Once the prayers had begun, they tore off their robes and cried out to the people, exhorting them to give up the cult of Satan and embrace the True Faith, Christianity. As expected, the Sultan had them beheaded the same day, in front of the entrance to the mosque – the famous Mezquita, which had been a pagan temple under the Romans, a Christian church under the Visigoths, and would once more become a Cathedral three centuries later. Rogelio – as well as some fifty other slain monks and nuns - became a legend and was consecrated, after the Moors were driven out of Granada by the Christians, as the patron saint of Montefrio's neighbour Illora, the ancient *Illurque* of the Romans... A statue of him now graces a plaza in the town, and his feast day is fervently celebrated every summer, with a holy procession.

Here he is, standing on his mountain…

To keep things in proportion, it should be said that in the 9th century the Moorish sultans were still relatively permissive of both Christianity and Judaism. The Arabs were still in a minority in Spain and they logically did their best not to incite the old-timers. What touched off the mozarabic rebellion in Cordoba was not that Christians were being persecuted, but that they resented that growing numbers of Christians, for reasons of survival, were converting to Islam under the constant pressure. According to Church documents of the time, they particularly objected to the noise the Muslims made proclaiming their faith, with bitter complaints about the *muezzins*, who screamed and shrieked like "madmen" five times a day from their towers. And as so often happens between neighbours who despise each other, "push came to shove"…

THE ROMAN MILLS

The Roman fortress in the Peñas de los Gitanos overlooked and protected the roads, farms and mills of the valley, all of which were built over the centuries in which the Empire regarded *Betis* – the southernmost province of Spain and the richest in natural resources – not only as a source of precious minerals but also as an enormous bread basket. However, in Parapanda Valley – which there is reason to believe is the site of the settlement designated as "Hipponova" in a document of the period – the Romans found something much rarer than fertile land to grow wheat: a deep, well-watered gorge near the source of the grain itself, ideally suited for the construction of mills. The fact that the grain for these mills came from all over the region is proven by the presence of the Roman bridge over the River Milanos, on the road built to transport the harvests, both from the wheatlands of the upper plateau on which Montefrio stands, and those of the region's main farming area, the Vega, or plain, below.

The basin of Parapanda Valley sheds water into a deep gorge, which drops sharply over several miles, between the floor of Parapanda Valley and the Plain of Granada, at 900 and 700 yards respectively. By diverting the water from the river bed along relatively short channels and aqueducts, the Romans could keep the wells, or "penstocks", of each of the six successive mills – which formed six "water steps" – full, and these columns of water created the pressure needed to turn the wheels beneath them.

When I say that there were six mills, I am going on the word of the local farmers, who tell me that, apart from the two which are still more or less intact, the ruins of four others exist further down in the gorge, which I have not yet explored for myself. I have, however, made out the remains of one other such mill, in the village itself. To see it, cross the bridge at the top of El Paseo and look at the house overhanging the other side of the gorge. The terrace is built on the top of a tall, square column of roughly-hewn stones, with the two characteristic drainage arches at the bottom, although these are hidden by the vegetation. It is identical in design to those of the Arroyo de los Molinos.

It is my belief that these mills were, since the Romans colonized Spain and until the definitive arrival of the industrial era – which, in southern Spain, did not occur until the 20th century - the driving force of Montefrio's economy. It isn't too far-fetched to say that without them – and, consequently, without the gorge's ideal hydraulic conditions – the town as we know it today would never have come into being. The old people of the Montefrio still remembered, at the end of the 20th century, how busy and crowded the gorge was in their youth, with its *fábricas de pan*, or "bread factories", since each mill had its oven as well. They described how, early every morning, mules laden with warm loaves wended their way up the valley and over the hill into Montefrio. Later, when electricity made it cheaper to grind the wheat with machines in the town – such as the *La Máquina* installed in the old Franciscan convent - the mills were gradually abandoned.

Since I first published this book, experts in mills and archaeology, and people simply interested in the history of technology, have come to Montefrio to visit the gorge, and they largely support my belief that the mills were built by the Romans. It is true that this model, known in Spain as the *molino de cubo* or "tank mill", after being invented by the Romans, was copied in water-poor areas such as ours down through the ages, only becoming obsolete, as I have said, with the advent of electricity. But in Montefrio there is the tell-tale proximity of the Roman fort looking down on the mills, and the Roman road leading away from them towards the village...

Diagrams of the Roman mills

This diagram shows how the water was captured from the tiny stream and deviated to fill the penstocks. It drained from either side of the valley, as we see above, and then flowed steeply down through the gorge – Arroyo de los Molinos – where the mills used it one after the other.

Before the stream reached each mill, some of its precious water was, by means of a sluice gate, made to flow, as horizontally as possible, along the slope in a trough until it rose high enough above the bottom of the gorge to flow across the aqueduct and fill the penstock. When the column was full, the water was released and turned the bladed wheel which set the millstones in motion.

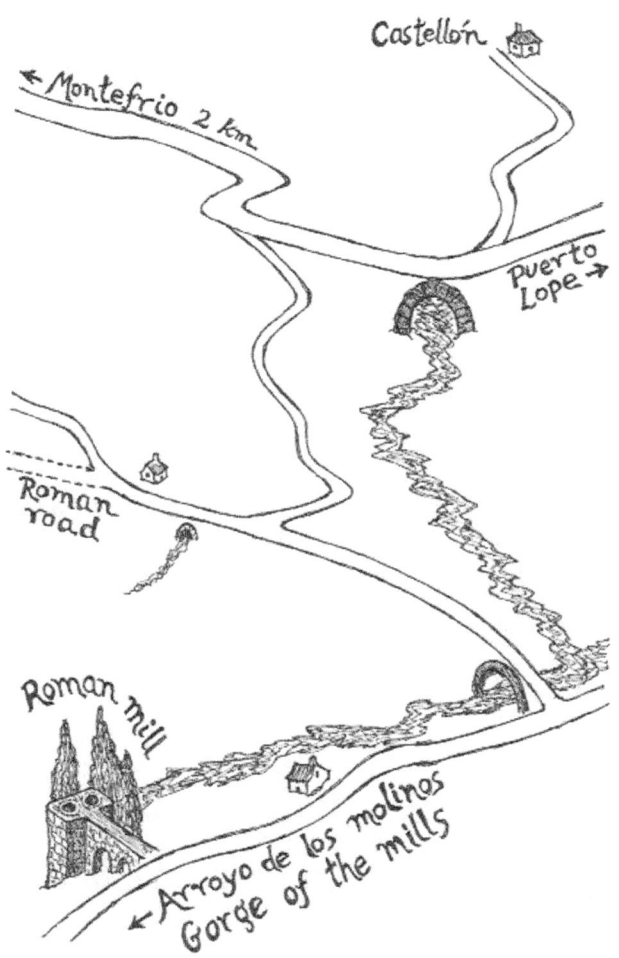

The *"Molino de Peinado"*

For years, on my afternoon walks in the gorge – and before I began to take an active interest in the village's history - I wondered what the strange-looking ruin could be, lying just below the road, next to the stream, with its two picturesque arches and narrow "bridge" leading out from the hillside to join the solid stone column standing all on its own, among the wild fig trees and poplars. None of the old-timers in the village seemed to know it even existed, so I took a closer look and realized that it could only have been a mill.

Before we carefully cross the narrow aqueduct, we can see the remains, largely lost in the bushes of the slope, of the stone-lined channel which drew water several hundred yards upstream. The aqueduct itself has lost its trough, but, according to Ulysses, the surface is covered with the cracked remains of a type of clay the Romans are known to have used to waterproof their hydraulic systems.

The most impressive part of the mill are its twin penstocks, the interior of which is formed of superimposed rings of stone, each one carved out of a single block over a meter wide. The sluice gates which sent the water into one or the other of these reservoirs are also the work of experienced engineers, carved with precision and elegance. The holding tanks were kept brim full in order to maintain constant pressure on the jet of water which was released at the bottom, turning a wheel fitted with small wooden blades, which in turn moved the horizontal mill stone. Alfonso Mazuela, who until his dying breath faithfully guarded the church of La Villa, told me that while the second mill of the gorge still operated, the jet of water which it produced was powerful enough "to go through a man's body". My dear friend's boyhood memories may have become exaggerated with time, but when a tower of water eight meters high escapes through a hole no wider than a child's wrist, the resulting jet could wound a man, if not perforate him.

If we walk around the mill, on the riverside, we can see the two drainage arches which released the used water into the stream.

The Roman road

We know that fragments of a Roman road were found on the other side of the mountain, near Alomartes, but there was no proof of its continuation through Montefrio, thus linking it with our Roman bridge in the Milanos Valley... until the day of the infamous official visit of the professor from Granada. While the dignitaries were examining the mill – on the subject of which, with her usual discretion, the lady preferred not to make any declarations which might compromise her professional reputation – a farmer came up and told us that there was a "strange road" on the other side of the stream which we might like to see. I wanted to follow him immediately, but one of our older school teachers doubted that a peasant could be trusted to distinguish antiquities and opined that it was not worthwhile, so we went straight to the restaurant, where the professor was honoured with an excellent lunch. The reader will already have guessed the rest: the next morning I was back to get the man out of his house, and 15 minutes later, found myself in front of 100 meters of genuine Roman road, identical to the segment of Alomartes!

At the last bend in the road, before the final stretch down towards the bridge, there is a very track rough leading off to the right (you may prefer to park here and go on foot). After several hundred yards you will pass a farmhouse on your right. Just beyond this point, you will observe how the road you are on forks in two. The current road is in fact a deviation from the original one, taking a more gentle slope up the hill beyond, whereas the old Roman road continues straight up the hill, at a much sharper angle.

The principle is the same as the Camino Medieval, which we walked on the Castillón Hill, except that here, because we are in open country, a supportive "cradle" was created with wedge-like upright slabs half-buried in the earth, to keep the flagstones from spreading. I still find it astonishing, knowing my neighbours as I do, that such a long stretch of paving in the middle of the fields, having been superseded by the new dirt road and forming a considerable obstacle to farming operations, should have escaped the bulldozers.

Each time I visit it, however, I notice how it is being slowly covered in earth and weeds, so as to be, in some places, almost invisible.

It is not worth continuing down the gorge only to see the second mill, since the interesting parts of it have been covered by a construction of more recent vintage, but many of my summer guests are attracted by the secluded pond in the stream, covered by a dense canopy of leaves and filled by a tiny waterfall, where, in the old days before swimming pools, the local boys used to skinny dip on hot August afternoons. Now it is almost always empty, especially if you go in the mornings, since the locals only enjoy bathing when the sun is at its most unbearable zenith.

The Roman Bridge

Ancient texts speak of a Roman road which came from the port now called Almuñécar, crossed the plain of Granada, ran up through the Gorge of the Mills and passed through the current site of Montefrio and the Milanos Valley, ending in Priego, on the way to Cordoba. Three traces of this road survive, the fragment of Alomartes on the plain, the one I discovered in Parapanda Valley, and the bridge of Milanos Valley. Until quite recently it was almost completely covered in dried mud, but now it has been cleared away and we can admire this charming construction which, with its single arch, has been called the smallest Roman bridge in Spain.

To get there, take the road to Algarinejo, towards the west, and immediately after crossing the modern bridge over the Milanos River, turn right on the dirt road. The Roman bridge - known as *el puente romano* - is 300 yards upstream.

The meaning of the name of the stream and its valley has intrigued historians. A *milano* is a sort of swallow, but ancient deeds of title, and even some 20th century old-timers of Montefrio, call the place not Milanos but *Vilanos*, which suggests that Milanos is in fact the corruption of a Latin-derived medieval name, which refers not to swallows but to the farmers or "villains" – the inhabitants of the Roman *villae* – who lived in this fertile valley. Our modern definition of "villain" comes from the fact that in Antiquity field workers were despised as uncouth brutes, quite the contrary of today's distinguished, and often English, "villa dwellers"!

The "Mountain Which Gives Bread"

The name of the rock mountain – *la Sierra de Parapanda* – which, at its 1,602 meters, towers over this fertile valley, shows us how highly valued these lands were. When the region was taken over, at the end of the 15th century, by King Ferdinand and Queen Isabella, they enjoined the peasants who came with them to plant wheat to feed the troops, wherever it would grow, *hasta en el monte, que para pan ha de dar –* "even on the mountainside, which will give bread". The orders were followed and, inspired by the historic phrase, the mountain has been called ever since *"para pan da"*, which translated literally as *"it gives bread"*.

My photos of Montefrio

This photo was taken above the village with Pepe Avila, the man who first sent me to Montefrio in the summer of 1960, and Cristóbal, the baker who was also a flamenco singer. I'm the lanky gringo holding the donkey's ear. I would have lost the picture altogether had not Cristóbal himself faithfully kept it on the wall of his tiny house for twenty years, and given it to me when I at last returned!

Delivering bread to the farms around Montefrio in 1961.
From left to right, myself, Pepe Avila and Cristóbal Moya,
with his horse and mule

Atop the Alhambra Castle, when I was studying in Granada the following winter, with the city's Moorish quarter, El Albaicin, below. You can see Parapanda Mountain, the great grey hump looming on the horizon just behind my shirt-collar…

Granada, winter of 1961

…and the next summer, up a fig tree in Manolo's orchard, devouring a ripe fig!

Cloister of the restored Franciscan convent, with belfry of the Church of San Antonio de Padua.

Abandoned crypts of the Old Cemetery, at the foot of the cliff of La Villa.

Poblado del Castillón and Gorge of the Mills, seen between the mountains.

Juan with his goats, with in the background the Cortijo del Castillón, and the trees of the Hill to the right.

Castillón – the olive oil mill

Juan with goats, and my Montefrio mongrel in the foreground

The supplies "pulley", with the Gran Calle below

Ulysses and the Roman fort of Los Castillejos…

Castillón – the cart road carved in the cliff face.

Poblado of the Castillón, with Sierra de Parapanda

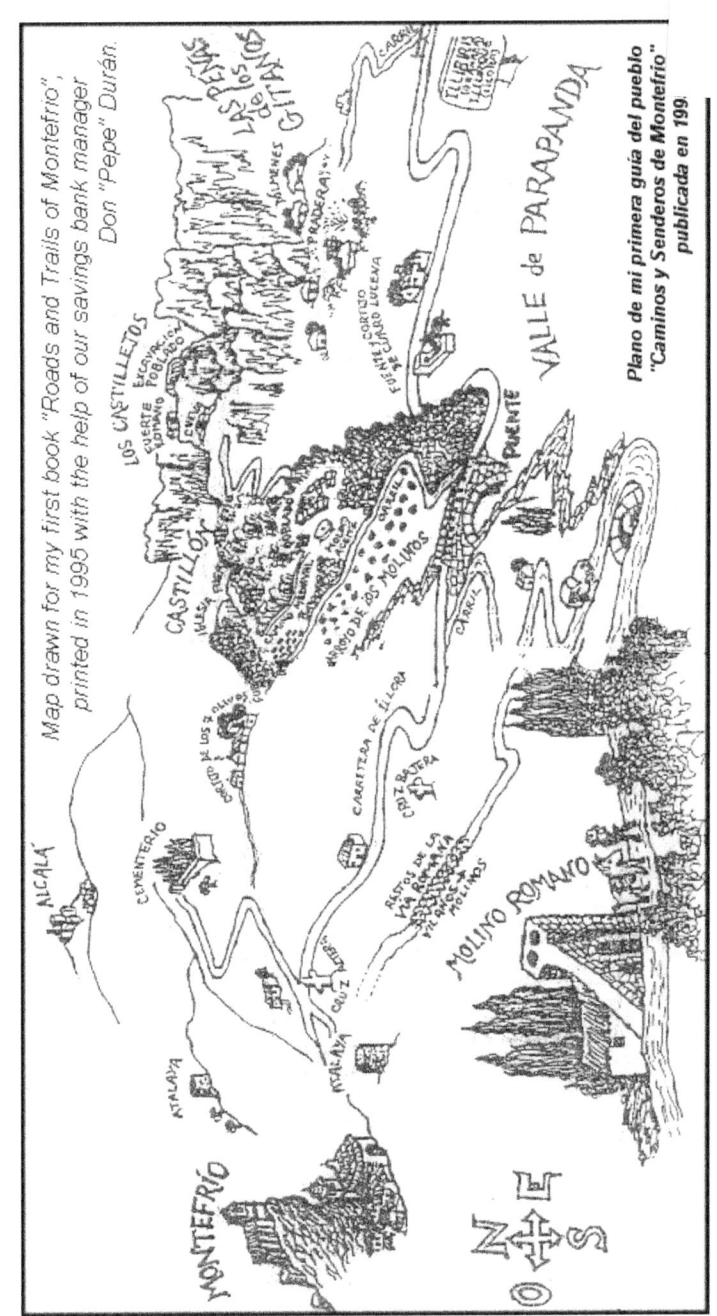

Map drawn for my first book "Roads and Trails of Montefrío", printed in 1995 with the help of our savings bank manager Don "Pepe" Durán.

Plano de mi primera guía del pueblo "Caminos y Senderos de Montefrío" publicada en 199.

Eight stories from Lorenzo's life in Montefrio, between the years 1960 and 1990

Montefrio, Last Stop

People often ask how I wound up living in a village in which I'm the only foreigner among some 8,000 Andalucians, and consequently far removed from the sophisticated international atmosphere of Marbella, Almuñecar and Mojácar. I answer that whenever I get bored (which is only now and then) I drive down to Granada, where I mingle with Frenchmen, Dutchmen, Muslims, Buddhists, tourists and artists, and even with other Englishmen in cultural exile such as myself. I have lunch in a Moroccan restaurant in the Albaicin, I admire the beautiful women for whom Granada is famous and then I go back happily to my olive trees, to my view of Parapanda Mountain and to the goatherd's daily visits (when he drives his goats out from the village and when he drives them back). The dirt track which leads to my *cortijo*, when wet, resembles a film about the Vietnam war, but I have a Russian jeep which can drive its way up just about anything but the olive trees themselves, as well as two phone lines (for voice calls and fax) strung on the 22 wooden poles which a spinsterly lady at the phone company, whom I wisely invited to lunch, had put in just for me. I recently hooked up to the Internet too, so I'm not as isolated from the "world" as one might imagine.

But when I first came to the village, 35 years ago, things were very different. The Montefrio of those days was similar to a present-day North African village - women in black, almost total public absence of girls of marrying age, thin boys with short pants and big eyes, mules, flocks of goats, dust, one or two cars and a decrepit bus which came and went to Granada, as the only sign that anything else existed outside of the village. They didn't even have television, unimaginable as this seems today: when a teacher friend of mine recently mentioned the fact to his media-conscious pupils with their psychedelic T-shirts and astronaut-sized track shoes, one asked him in amazement, "How could you live?".

But they did have flamenco. A few days after I arrived in Madrid from New York, at the beginning of the summer, I heard a conference about *cante hondo* at the students' residence where I was boarding; I later asked the young speaker where I could hear flamenco in its natural setting rather than in a concert hall. He told me about a great but little-known singer who was the butcher of his village in Andalucia and I decided to pay him a visit that August.

In the long run, Montefrio turned out to be by far the most crucial event of that summer for me, but when I was living it all, my discovery of the village represented only one fascinating revelation among half a dozen others. I was 18, poetic-looking, and I nurtured, let us say, a rather high opinion of myself by comparison with the rest of humanity - an appraisal, which, thus far, has only been partially borne out, and I'm already 53. *C'était la jeunesse!*

For me, the summer of 1960 didn't begin in Montefrio but in Pamplona, with the memory of *The Sun Also Rises* still palpitating in my memory. Three of us went there from Madrid on a tiny motor scooter with sidecar: myself, a Swede and a Spanish student from La Mancha, who was the owner of the vehicle. We unrolled our sleeping bags in a grove of trees on the bank of a river near the town, we filled our leather wine-skins with red wine (at 6 pesetas per liter) in the bodegas and went dancing through the streets, each with a red kerchief tied around his throat. We fell in with a Parisian hitchhiker who looked like Gérard Philippe and who engaged a bull in some serious capework in the midst of the stampede, using his windbreaker. When they let him out of jail, after the festival was over, I joined my new and fascinating friend, who like me was in love with literature and travel, and we set out together on the road of the summer bullfight festivals, the *ferias taurinas*.

Since Yves was travelling with a very small amount of money, we hitch-hiked, although in real terms it was not that much cheaper than taking the train. *Auto-stop*, as the French dubbed it, was very fashionable then among young people of our ilk. You felt proud of every mile you travelled at someone else's expense, and it was almost a point of honour not to give up and take the train. In those years there was still very little traffic on Spain's highways, and I frequently felt like "throwing in the towel" and paying, but my friend, who had even hitch-hiked through Yugoslavia, had his principles and would not allow it.

The same applied to food: with ridiculously cheap restaurants everywhere, we had to live on tins of sardines with bread and tomatoes, because Yves felt that eating in restaurants was only for the *bourgeois*.

But in spite of the somewhat austere conditions imposed by my friend, it was a thrilling trip.

In fact, I had already done some hitch-hiking of my own that summer. At the end of the fiesta Javier decided that his scooter wouldn´t make it back to Madrid with such a heavy load, and the Swede and I drew straws to see which man would have to hit the road on his own. I was especially annoyed to lose because I had been sold a pair of prettily coloured birds by a street peddler and, never having hitch-hiked before, wondered if anyone would take a man with a cage in his hand. The Swede promised to cover the price of the train ticket if I was forced to pay to get to Madrid, and they left me on the outskirts of Pamplona. Tired of waiting in the shade of a tree for several hours without seeing more than a few cars, I began to walk. At the end of the hot, dusty day a tractor took me as far as the next station town where I got on board a train to Zaragoza, sitting on a bare wooden bench among field workers dressed in corduroys and caps, who shared with me their dinner of potato omelette and red wine. A radio was broadcasting a speech by a spokesman of the Franco regime, which went on and on bombastically, and seeing the peasants long-suffering expressions I could not repress an ironic comment, saying *"Habla habla habla y no dice nada* - He talks, talks, talks and says nothing". I was rewarded with a few sympathetic glances, but a man in a suit on the other side of the aisle, obviously a member of the winning side in the war, threateningly called me to order and said I should respect the government of the country I was visiting. All the eyes of the peasants sunk to the floor... In Zaragoza I got a night train to Madrid, with more wooden benches, and was so tired when I reached my rooms on the Calle de los Madrazo that when I awoke 12 hours later I found that I had wetted the bed! The Swede apologetically paid me back, but when the maid put a bowl of water in the cage so the birds could bathe, I was dismayed to find that they were only greyish brown swallows.

A few days later, my new hero, Yves, knocked on the door of my flat, having just been released from jail with the many other infractors of the rule against fighting the bulls of the *encierro*, and bringing with him some spectacular photos of his feat taken by a local photographer, which he had found posted on the front of a souvenir shop. Yves had been in Spain several times before so we spoke Spanish together, since I only had basic knowledge of French. To while away the many hours we had to spend waiting for rides, we sang the songs we knew to one another, and when we had exhausted our repertory of blues, fandangos and Spanish Civil War music, he introduced me to the ironically wistful ballads of George Brassens, then at the height of his popularity in France. He wrote down the lyrics on a notebook propped on his backpack, and I sang along imitating the sounds, although many of the words and expressions were strange to me. The day came when Yves no longer seemed so heroic to me and we fell out, but I owe much to him for the pleasure which that most subtle of languages has given me since - the kind of debt one is more willing to acknowledge in retrospect than in the thick of emotions...

In Valencia, followed the rise of the prodigy of Pamplona, the boyish Paco Camino, and we even saw him rise in the real sense of the word as well. It was one of the truly unforgettable moments of my bullfighting years. Camino was "dedicating" his bull to the sunny (and cheap) side of the plaza (where, of course, we were sitting with our wine-skins) when the bull, which had been standing as still as a statue at the other side of the ring, suddenly began to run towards him, like a noiseless locomotive. Camino did not realize that the public's frantic screams were meant to warn him of the impending disaster, and he went on smiling and waving his hat, until the bull's broad horns neatly surrounded his waist. Aghast, we saw him twirl up in the air exactly like a rag doll, with the smile still on his lips. Camino was even elegant when the bull threw him, and a few weeks later he had recovered from his bruises and was killing again, elegantly.

Each day after the fight we took the tramway to a beach near the city. A fisherman and his son cooked for us on a fire in a hole in the sand, and when night fell we unrolled our sleeping bags close down to the water, where, after a first night of torture, we discovered that the mosquitoes wouldn't bother us. Spain was still a very prudish country then, and there were signs warning the visiting northern women against wearing *trajes de baño de dos piezas*, two-pieced bathing suits, not foreseeing the day when the rule would be followed to the letter by simply forgetting one of the pieces!

It took us three days to get from Valencia to Malaga, since not many drivers were willing to take two giants with knapsacks aboard their tiny SEAT 600's. We passed the Peñón de Ifach, dwarfing its coastline of poor, whitewashed houses, and the fishing village of Benidorm, which resembled some Greek island washed up on the shore of the shining sea. By the evening of the first day we were in Huercal Overa, where the sidewalks were so clean that we unrolled our sleeping bags to spend the night on one, until a pair of Civil Guardsmen invited us to sleep in the jail, which was just as clean and empty as the sidewalk.

By the afternoon of the second day we were in the sugar cane fields of Salobreña. The village on its hump of rock glistened in the sun like a citadel of The Thousand and One Nights. After waiting for several hours without luck, we decided to give up and continue the next day. There was no one there except the local people, and the streets seemed to have been carved out of snow, radiant with sea-blue light. Our enchantment was such that we had to touch the whitewashed walls and steps and fountains to be sure they were not the product of a mirage; and at the top of the hill stood the Moorish castle, squat and solid like a great lump of brown sugar half-melted by the sun. The owner of the only *pensión* told us that Cervantes had slept there, but what impressed us most was the old woman in black who sat all day in the crudely paved patio, without moving or speaking. But when she saw us cross the courtyard to go up to our room with our tins of sardines, tomatoes and bread, thus avoiding the gloomy (and for Yves, *bourgeois*) dining room, she raised her black-hooded head and gave out a piercing, wailing cry, directed at no one in particular except, perhaps, at God to tell him that the barbarians ate bread and sardines just like any *cristiano*: *Van a co-MER. ¡VAN A CO-MER!* (They're going to eat!).

In those days, bullfighting was highly fashionable among artists and intellectuals, largely due to the writings of Hemingway and the paintings of Picasso, and Torremolinos was the in place to stay for the happy few. All the jet-setting *aficionados* gathered there, although Hemingway himself was absent, since his last summer in Spain was the previous one, which he christened "The Dangerous Summer". But, strangely, there was someone whom the Spaniards called "*el falso Hemingway*", an eccentric American millionaire who resembled him, when seen from a distance of about 20 yards, which was enough - in the absence of the real thing - for all the newspapers to write about him incessantly. (This character had a peculiar hobby: he travelled around the capitals of the world looking for strange names - for example, he told me that he had discovered, in the Civil Registry of Caracas, that someone had christened his child with the name of... Jesus Lenin!). Inevitably, there was also the rich, spoiled American girl who followed the bullfighters rather than the bullfights themselves; ours was called Virginia and she drove from one fair to the other in an expensive car stalking her prey.

I have to admit that the Hemingway look-alike left me as cold as a dish of leftover *paella*, that the torero-crazy Virginia struck me as being spoiled and vulgar, and that even Orson Welles - whom I later recognized for the genius which he was - only caught my attention because, the day his massive bulk lumbered up to the table we were sharing with "Hemingway" at a sidewalk café in Valencia, Yves gazed at him as if he were a living legend. Sadly, Welles was always more admired in Europe than in his native land, and I was coming from North America. I was not to discover *Citizen Kane* and *The Lady From Shanghai* until later, in the student cinemas of the Latin Quarter.

No - the great celebrity of the summer for me was a Frenchman, with whom I was well familiar thanks to my artistic mother: the poet, painter and (most of all) great personality Jean Cocteau, only three years before his death. He was staying in Torremolinos where, a few days after our meeting, a Civil Guardsman caught him behind a boat on the sand doing "something" with a fisherman, as a result of which he spent a few days in jail until the French authorities could come to the rescue of their *grand homme*. We saw him in the lobby of the Hotel Miramar, where the bullfighters stayed, impeccably elegant in his dark blue suit, his shirt and tie as perfect and natural as if he had been born in them, and his impish, bird-like face framed by a crown of frizzy grey hair.

Unfortunately I still did not speak enough French to follow the lively conversation which ensued, and had to make do with the running translation which Yves gave me in our common language, Spanish. When Cocteau heard that we were sleeping in the ruins of the Moorish castle, he vehemently declared that he hated hotels and wished he could spend the night up on the Gibralfaro with us, *à la belle étoile*. A group photo was taken, with Cocteau in the centre, flanked on one side by Yves and the other by me, the false Hemingway, the prissy Virginia looking a bit like Elizabeth Taylor, plus a very serious American bullfighter whose name I have forgotten but who in his old age became a painter of bullfighting scenes. When the photographer fired his flash bulb, Cocteau sprang up into the air and cried joyously, "Jack in the box!". I asked him to dedicate a few lines to my mother on the hotel stationery to send for her birthday the next month, and he sketched one of his famous faun's heads, wreathed with his whimsical hand-writing, which was a drawing in itself.

There was an interval of a week or so before the bullfight fair of Bilbao, with the whole of Spain in the middle. The magic combination of elements, like Lorca's "living coin", would never occur again: extreme youth, thirst for adventure and enough time and money to wander at will, in a country which in many ways was still the *vieja España* of Goya, where you still had the feeling that you were discovering things for the first time - and sometimes actually were! Travelling through Spain, in those days, was not only a trip in the geographical sense, but a journey into the past.

I regret to say that I remember nothing of my first visit to the Alhambra, for the simple reason that I have visited it so often since then. From Granada, we went to the village recommended by my friend Pepe Avila. Due to the almost total absence of traffic off the main roads, we were forced to take the train to El Tocón on the plain, at the foot of the *montes* or hills, where a bus was waiting which carried us, along with a small group of wrinkled men dressed in grey and wrinkled women dressed, almost all of them, in black, up to the village.

When you approach Montefrio from El Tocón you get the most surprising view of all. The village is sunk in a valley among the hills, but the church and ruined castle are perched high up on a great spur of rock, so the first thing one sees as the bus descends is a lonely bell tower. A few dizzying curves later and the entire church emerges triumphantly from below, like a terra cotta man-of-war sailing over an undulating sea of olive groves. Little by little, at the foot of the spur, the tiled houses of the village come into view, dazzling whitely in the cleft between two ochre hills...

I remember like a welcoming angel the old man who had been sent to fetch us at the bus stop in front of the big, round church. With his beret, waistcoat, cheery toothless smile and cigarette butt stuck to his lip, he resembled a character in that classic of Spanish cinema, "*Bienvenido Mister Marshall*". Crowds of women and children gathered in front of us in the street to stare, since they had never seen a foreigner before, so that Tio Paco had to open a path among them for us to pass.

He took us straight to the local Casino, where the "flamenco boys" - the fabulous butcher Manuel Avila, the baker Cristobal Moya, who delivered his bread to the farms with a mule, the two gypsy brothers Melchor and José and the barber, Rafael, who played the guitar - were waiting around a table loaded with glasses of white wine (only women drank beer in Spain then) and a bowl of *pipirranas*, a juicy tomato salad, and *mollejas*, chunks of sheep entrails fried in oil and garlic. Three or four hours later we were taken, half-drunk, to Pepe's house, which he had instructed to be made ready for us, and where we fell asleep in front of a noisy electric fan, which someone had thoughtfully put in the bedroom.

And the next day we were gone, heading for new adventures. But an olive seed had taken root in my heart.

The House at the Corner of Jesus

My official reason for coming to Spain, when I asked Dad to finance the endeavour, was that I wanted to study "hispanic culture", which I naively thought of as flamenco singing and the poetry of Lorca and Saint John of the Cross. But I soon realized that these subjects had never existed in the curriculum of the *Facultad de Filosofía y Letras*. Flamenco, in those patrician days, was looked down on as uncouth music for gypsies, nighthawks and left-wing intellectuals, which seemed shocking then although I am now inclined to believe that it was better that way. Lorca, being associated with the other political gang, the "reds", was never mentioned in public, and his books, all printed in Argentina, were only sold under the counter. And the *erótico-místico* San Juan was clearly out of line with the lofty, moralistic image of Christianity defended by Franco's totalitarian regime.

For me, after New York in the "beatnik" years, the atmosphere of the university was stifling, almost medieval. My classmates were nuns, priests and - for the large part - well-off Spanish *señoritas* who were preparing to be schoolteachers, one of whom, I confess, I almost immediately fell in love with. We only studied the thinkers whose ideas were approved by the *Opus Dei*, a powerful Catholic organization to which most of the professors belonged - these were frightening people, who had highly intellectual, beautifully constructed, hermetically sealed arguments to support every one of their positions. This explains why I spent much more time in the bars around the Plaza Mayor carousing with my friends from the student residence, and trying to get together privately with my young *madrileña*, than bothering about school.

One specific impediment to academic success was the great trouble I had with the Latin, both because the Spanish students were already well advanced in this subject from their secondary studies and, also, because being a dead tongue it had no appeal for me whatsoever. A sympathetic young priest in the class offered to coach me at home in his dimly-lit flat, and we spent long hours (or at least, they seemed long to me) reading the Wars of Gaul around the *mesa de camilla*, a round table with a brazier of smoldering embers underneath, roasting the lower parts of our bodies and trying to warm the upper ones, the parts which couldn't be covered with the heavy *manta* or tablecloth, by swallowing the thimblefuls of brandy served by his old mother. But I feel sure that Joaquin's kind help would not have been enough to save me from being flunked, even if I had stayed on to take the end-of-year exams.

After that disheartening autumn, I spent the Christmas holidays deliciously with Yves, my companion of the summer's bullfighting adventures, in a picturesque garret "under the roof" of a sombre old building north of the Place de la République. It was my first visit to France and by time I said farewell to his working class family, well-stuffed with oysters, *foie gras* and *steak frites*, I realized that my life, to paraphrase Josephine Baker, would be divided between two loves, Spain and Paris.

Back in my apartment near the Paseo del Prado (for I had soon moved out of the uncomfortable student residence) I began to realize the mistake I had made. Madrid was really just another hard, grey city, which somehow refused to render up its soul, if it had one. The mysterious Pilar, although lovelier to behold and better groomed than my Greenwich Village girlfriends, was also much less adventurous, and as for my studies, it was pretty clear that all they were being good for was to keep my monthly allowance of 75 Canadian dollars rolling in. This amount was then enough for me to live like a *señorito*, ordering tailor-made suits, taking taxis everywhere and standing my friends from the Residence to drinks when they were out of pocket, which was most of the time. May my dear Dad forgive me, but I had decided that I could learn much more about hispanic culture in bars than at school. As for the sacrosanct degrees and diplomas, it was possible, in those faraway years when there were less young people than jobs, to feel that I was smart enough to get along in life without them.

Therefore, with nary a thought for the academic consequences of my rash act, I transferred to the University of Granada at the beginning of the spring, in the middle of the first year of the Romance Languages course. That way I would be closer to Montefrio, the fascinating village I had discovered the previous summer, closer to flamenco, and closer to the spirit of my beloved poet Lorca.

Behind the splendour of its Moorish castle, Granada was only a sleepy provincial town, extremely conservative, and the Faculty of Letters, then housed in the 19th century palace which is now the School of Translation, was even worse than what I had left in Madrid. The fact that I was the only foreign student was sensational enough for the daily newspaper to interview and photograph me in my Byronesque black corduroy suit. I was asked about my interest in Montefrio, to the great satisfaction of the few villagers who read the paper, and also about my love of flamenco, which I rather eloquently defined as "man crying out in his solitude", *el grito del hombre en la soledad*. The reporter from *Patria* also mentioned that I had a "mane of hair like a torrent of gold". Although only moderately long by today's standards, back then it was enough to create a commotion wherever I went, even New York.

I chose to study Classical Arabic rather than Latin as the lesser of two evils, but the only thing I did successfully in that class was to copy the teacher's arabesques with great elegance, for which I was much praised, even though I had only the vaguest idea what I was writing. I must have gone to class about 20 times at the most.

As I would have easily foreseen if I had then had the self-knowledge I have since so painfully acquired, my assault on the Spanish University did not survive the spring, and I was soon chasing a more exciting, and above all more attainable, rainbow. At the beginning of the Semana Santa celebrations, in a tavern where she was surrounded by old men offering her wine, I met a tom-boyish German girl whom I immediately recognised as a kindred spirit. This fearless hitchhiker and dropout from the Munich art school was christened Leiselotte but insisted on being called only Lilo (pronounced LEE-lo), because her real name was too feminine. That same night I took her up to the Albaicin to see the sun rise over the Alhambra, and, a few days later, to Montefrio to hear my flamenco friends singing *saetas*, the heart-rending chants for the Easter passion. The fact that Manolo Avila was the most spiritual butcher in the history of music was especially evident when he stepped out on the balcony of the gentlemen's club, El Casino, with his grey jacket and white shirt buttoned to the throat, to solemnly salute the crucified Christ - whom he in many ways resembled, and not only when he was singing.

Lilo agreed with me that both Montefrio and Manolo were unique, and after endless conversations and bottles of wine, shared on the mattress on the floor of the tiny house I was renting on the Calle Padre Alcover, we decided to spend the summer in the village, and then go together to study in Paris, I at the Sorbonne and she in the atelier of a painter I knew of, because my mother had studied with him several years before. That was how we lived then, making it up as we went along! I had had a taste of France and wanted more, and as for Spain, it would for many years hence be that archaic and romantic country to which I would travel as a pilgrim whenever I could.

We hitch-hiked to Paris to make arrangements for our studies in the autumn and returned to Montefrio, where we found a house to stay in until September. It was as graceful and tall as a tower of the Generalife, the summer palace of the Alhambra, with a similar "mirador" on top, with three whitewashed Moorish arches in each side. Embedded in the corner of the massive house, behind an iron grill, was a framed engraving of the Cristo de Moclín, for which they called the place "The Corner of Jesus". This image of Christ carrying the Cross, the original of which is in the nearby town of Moclín, is said to miraculously help childless women who pray before it to become pregnant, and as such it is mentioned in Lorca's tragedy *Yerma*, "Barren".

We had to go to Cordoba to settle the deal with the owner, who ran a boarding house for construction workers. There, across a round white plastic table cover, we agreed to pay a monthly rental of 650 pesetas, which was about $10 and seemed to us ridiculously cheap, although the neighbours later told us we could have got it for half the price. Then the fierce looking, but somehow very likeable woman handed us a heavy key, as if we were crusaders setting out to liberate the Temple of Jerusalem. The only condition was that we could not use the parlour and bedroom on the ground floor, where she kept her belongings, and where she stayed a week in August to take part in the village *fiesta*.

Since we spent most of our time high up in the tower painting and writing, we found the few days of her interesting presence enjoyable. She was a stout peasant woman with a faint moustache who dressed, of course, in black, and had a very small one-legged husband. She told us that when the other women teased her for having such a physically reduced husband, she would put them in their places by retorting, "Maybe, but he has a 'cigar' like this!", raising her forearm and gripping it at the elbow. She made a point of telling us that there were some *malas mujeres* in the town who were much visited by the other husbands, but that hers had enough to keep him busy at home.

The villagers still remember this amazon, who died suddenly of a stroke a few years later in a train station in France, where she had gone to visit a relative, by her curious nickname: *La Barranquilla*. This was the result of a humorous association between the title of a Colombian ditty one often heard on the radio about an alligator which makes a trip to that town, and the fact that, before she moved to Cordoba, she had owned a bar (hence: *bar*-ranquilla). But her real name was Antonia, although, as usual, no one used it except when addressing her personally. In a town where everyone is named after one of a handful of popular saints, the pseudonym or *apodo* is the only way of effectively identifying one Antonio and Antonia, and Paco and Paquita, from the other.

Lilo and I were a great novelty and friends came and went all day long to see us, but the one I especially associate with the house itself was a blacksmith known as Pepe Sena. He worked with his father in a forge on the Calle Baja which reminded me of Vulcan´s furnace, where I would often go to hear Pepe talk in his lisping *granadino* drawl as he plucked the glowing horseshoes and farm tools out of the embers and hammered them into shape. Montefrio has always had at least one specimen in residence of the type I call "philosophers", men who in spite of their rough trades and rural upbringing have done some reading and take a keen interest in the world outside, even though, in those years before television, they gave the impression of looking at it through the wrong end of a telescope. And these village dreamers inevitably gravitate towards the visitor in their midst, not so much to question him - and in our case her as well, because Pepe was especially fond of Lilo - about the democratic traditions of northern Europe and the monuments of the *ciudad luz* but, rather, to hold forth on these subjects themselves, in their jumbled-up way. One of the many ironies one discovers as a travelller is that the only people who ask one questions about the far-away places one has visited are those who have already travelled themselves.

Pepe was a tall and handsome man, with a swarthy, hawkish face like a Moor, and he would come around after the day's work to converse, and give us all sorts of often useful advise. But the best thing he taught us was how to cook lamb kidneys in white wine sauce, a popular dish called *riñones al Jerez*. I can still see him under the naked light bulb stirring the thick gravy made of fried bread and wine – we never used real sherry as the name demanded – with the glistening crescents of meat bobbing up to the surface everywhere. It is definitely the best way to serve kidneys and I remember the dear man, who some years later went to Madrid to manufacture tourist souvenirs, copper lamps and ashtrays, every time, or almost every time, I serve the dish myself. The kitchen in the old houses of Montefrio always stands apart from the main building, in the corral or backyard, to keep out the smoke and fumes, because all the cooking was done on charcoal embers, which had to be lit with a ball of paper and then vigorously fanned.

It would be another 15 years before the village would have running water in the houses, and my sturdy companion Lilo had to fill our jugs and buckets at the fountain behind the house, all on her own since we were told that it would have been unthinkable for me, as a man, to assist her. In Montefrio then as today, there are *cosas que no se hacen* – some

89

things one just doesn't do. I remember seeing a man go back and forth with two buckets, because his wife was sick they said, but he did it after midnight when no one could see him.

It wouldn't have done to be mixed up with all those cackling women! High up in my tower I could see the sheet of water which splashed out of the clay jugs and flowed down through the Esquina de Jesus, and hear the stream of chatter produced by the *vecinas*, who seemed to talk just for the pleasure of creating a bridge of sound among one another. I still marvel at how the women of our village manage to think of so many things to say without ever communicating anything that could later possibly be held against them. It is part of the Mediterranean way of being, so different to the countries of the north, where people, when they meet, say precisely what they have to say, without embellishments, before going about their business.

The Butcher Who Sang Like a Bird

In spite of the rapid changes which were beginning to affect Spain in the early 1960's, Montefrio seemed timeless. Every time I came back from Paris there were the same smells of frying olive oil and goat droppings, and there were the same slippery pebbles on the streets, which swarmed with almost as many four-legged beasts as today, under their cover of cast concrete, they do with four-wheeled ones. There were also the threadbare little *fiestas* without truckloads of sound equipment, which one didn't have to be a progress-thirsty provincial to enjoy. But, for me, in my fascination with the eccentric and the bizarre, there was, first and foremost, Manolo.

Many people think of Manolo as a skilled and original singer, which he certainly was, but I remember him as a very special, and at the same time very Spanish, man. Other writers, describing him in his older and more glorious years, compared him to a "gnarled grape vine" and "a butcher who sang like a bird", and both images are appropriate. When my mother painted his picture, in the winter of 1960, he kept falling asleep, so she simply showed him with his eyes shut. Being naturally haggard and gaunt, the similarity with a corpse was not lost on anyone, especially the hyper-sensitive model himself. *"¡Me ha pintao muerto!"*, he would complain indignantly, for years after - "She painted me dead".

When I first came to Montefrio, he had his *carniceria* on the Calle Alta, in the place where there is now a shoe shop, at the corner with the Calle de Marquesas. There was no comparison with the hygienic, well-stocked butcher shops we have now, with their rosy pink pigs hanging in the cold room and their scales with digital screens, which give the exact price. Manolo's place, even in the relatively unsophisticated 60's, was a throwback to the Civil War, a sort of morgue for unrecognizable bits of stringy goat or sheep, depending on what he had culled from his flock the day before.

Every morning, a gaggle of housewives fingered and poked the bloody tissue which he hacked up at random and scattered on the counter. The din was constant: Manolo arbitrarily decided what each lump cost, but as soon as he shouted "*¡cinco pesetas!*" the interested party would scream back "*¡tres pesetas!*", and so on. Sometimes the argument became so heated that it almost seemed as if he would take his knife to the woman's throat.

But as soon as he noticed me step down from the street - his *amigo inglés, poeta y aficionado* - he would open both arms and throw back his head to toss off a bar of *cante hondo* and, projecting his voice over the uproar, resume the conversation we had left off the day before, as if nothing had happened since.

It was never a normal conversation, but a "Manolo conversation", which could leap suddenly, but somehow always gracefully, from Spain's downfall 300 years ago at the hands of guess-which-pirates, to his arthritis, to the greatest singer of all times (Manuel Torres, because he was dead - the greatest living one could only be himself). Then he would inevitably pause to remind me, the naive foreigner, of the fact that no one could be trusted, which sad state of affairs he expressed with a saying which may have been a Manolo original, and which, exceptionally, I shall leave untranslated, *Para conocerle a un hombre, hay que comerse un saco de sal.* If we were not overheard, he would bemoan the cruel injustice of not having been a *moro* with a harem of wives, forty of them to be precise. But then some gypsy matron would get hold of a mangled scrap of goat's liver and shout "*¡tres pesetas!*" and he plunged back into the fray, wild-eyed.

Other flamenco singers might have surpassed him in virtuosity, but none had the thrilling woody quality of Manolo's voice when, as he put it, he would *dar el cambio* or "make the change" from one register to the other. It was enough to give you goose-flesh, and Manolo himself would often hold out his skinny, veined forearm and pull back his sleeve so that I could witness the impressive number of bumps which were being produced by his own music. Like all true artists, he was all the audience he needed.

I took this photograph of Manolo singing up on the Calvario Hill, above the gypsy quarter, in 1961. He was wrapped up in his *bufanda* against the cold, although it may not have been cold at all, just another of his manias – to protect his vocal cords, he said. You can see that the cliff of La Villa is bare rock, since the pine trees weren't planted until a decade later, and the tower of the old church was still without its pointed roof.

What with all the current-day official encouragement (prizes, subsidies, razzmatazz), there are many professionally competent flamenco singers, but compared to Manolo the new breed seem more like vocal athletes than the wandering minstrel, the musical poet who was my friend. When I see them sitting on the brightly-lit festival stage or in the softly-lit TV studio, well-paid and well-fed, they remind me, with their prolonged bellows of simulated pain and their massive microphones, of someone at the dentist having a tooth pulled, or - as my father once joked - on the toilet suffering from constipation. Manolo softened his howls of despair with bitter-sweet irony, and gazed searchingly, almost pleadingly into your eyes, as if he were really trying to say something to you, something which could be expressed no other way than through his beloved *siguiriyas* and *soleares*.

It must be said that the lean, gritty atmosphere back then was so much more conducive to "natural" flamenco, the music of suffering par excellence. I recently heard a young *cantaor* whose car keys were fashionably dangling from his trouser pocket, as he sang a heart-rending *copla* about a man whose mother died unattended because he could not afford to call in the doctor. But with Manolo, every word was personally felt, even personally experienced: he had served in the Civil War with the Anarchists and spent the rest of his life herding goats and sheep over the hills of Montefrio - day-dreaming and singing as he went.

I would hang about outside until he closed up and went to the *matadero*, the village slaughterhouse, to get the next day's meat ready. It was a cavernous place, and in Manolo's hands what would normally have been a rather sorry scene took on airs of a pagan ritual. I wrote a long-since mislaid poem about it, speaking of him as a wizard or priest chanting as he sacrificed the lamb, although in reality Manolo just couldn't stop singing, whatever he was doing. The poem spoke of the little girl with long braids who came with a bucket to collect the entrails, which her mother cleaned out at a cement tank. When he was done, he carried the bucket home with the intestines and blood for Maria to make *morcilla* - black pudding - for the store. The lid of the bucket was turned upside down to hold the tastier bits of offal, such as the *mollejas* (sweetbreads) which we would take to my place for Lilo to fry up with olive oil and garlic, for our tapas. I can still see her fanning the charcoal embers under the big pan, while Manolo sang and I poured the white wine.

I did the drawing below much later in life, when I was the age Manolo was when I first knew him, and with our young gypsy guitarist Franci accompanying him in my farmhouse, but it gives you an idea of what we were up to in 1960 or so.

While this was being done, I was ordered to put on the record player. I had brought with me from New York a "portable" high-fi set, quite boxy and heavy, which created a sensation in the village, since none of the flamenco boys owned a machine on which to hear their favourite singers. I also brought from Madrid a long-playing record of the great singer Antonio Mairena, then at the peak of his career, which caused such a sensation that I had Manolo, Cristobal the baker and the two gypsy brothers, Melchor and José, knocking on the door at every odd moment asking to hear it once more. Once both sides had been solemnly heard, they would treat me to their own improvised concert, which was what I wanted.

93

After Manolo had listened to the record player and had his wine and *mollejas*, he would forget about going home for lunch and, what with the heat, fell asleep on the big straw-filled mattress we had spread on the floor. Soon he was snoring loudly and a cloud of black flies was hovering around each of his crumpled, smelly socks. Before long María would be wailing up from the street, *"Manolo, la comida, Manolo, la morcilla"*. She was less concerned about him missing lunch than the blood congealing before it went into her big iron pot on the hearth.

Many years later, when he began to win prizes and appear on TV, the villagers granted him a certain amount of respect, but back them he was just plain *loco perdío* for all but the handful of flamenco lovers. He had two qualities which are most rare among Iberian males, spontaneity and transparency, which is why they misunderstood him, and why I loved him.

I will close this tribute to my recently deceased friend with an anecdote which caused much grief at the time but which, many years later, he and I would often laugh about as the story of *"el tomate de la Lilo"*.

Lilo stormed out of his butcher shop one morning and marched up to me in the plaza, red-faced with Teutonic indignation. It seemed that instead of attending to her properly (as if he ever attended to anyone properly!), Manolo had looked over the contents of her shopping basket and casually taken out a large tomato, which he then proceeded to munch (something he was very fond of) as he unrepentantly turned back to his housewives. In retrospect it sounded silly, just another of Manolo's theatricals, but I was highly influenced by Lilo and her rigorous ideals of behaviour, and stormed into the shop, loudly accusing him of offending my *mujer*, in front of all of his amazed customers. I got some sharp words in reply, and went off.

I quickly cooled down and realized how stupid I had been, but the damage was done - I had made him lose face in front of "the others". When I saw him in the street, he turned his back on me, and I went home in absolute despair. This intolerable situation went on for several days; even Lilo, usually intransigent, realized that it had got out of hand. I wrote him a long letter begging for his forgiveness, and threatening to leave Montefrio immediately if he did not forget what had happened. I put the envelope under his door in the night.

The next morning I ran into him in the plaza, on the way home with his bucket of offal. With a distracted grin, he instantly picked up where our last conversation had left off... that is, the last conversation before the tomato.

In memoriam
Manuel Avila Rodriquez
1912 – 1993

Flamenco Summer

When I call the summer of 1961 flamenco, it isn't only because it was filled with the wonderful music itself - in the corner of a tavern, at the barber shop of Rafael (our only guitarist), or in the Moorish tower atop the ancient house in which we lived - but, rather, because the spirit of flamenco seemed to be present in everything. The word is sometimes used in Spanish to describe a person who is "fiery, passionate", and it is in this sense which I use it here.

In the morning Lilo would go down to buy milk from the goatherd who drove his flock through the streets - you gave him your saucepan and he milked a goat while you waited. But when we had been up all night with our moonlit *juergas* in the lookout tower, we would rise well after Francisco had gone past with his herd, and have our breakfast on the back porch of the Café Español, where there was a fig tree which seemed to be loaded with ripe fruit all summer long - *brevas* in July and *higos* in September. As we took our *café con leche*, the gypsy bootblack known to all as Culebra ("snake", perhaps because he had the low brow and beady eyes of a rattlesnake) would climb up the tree and pick a few handfuls of night-cool, purple-black figs for us to eat with our churros. In the days before everyone had fridges, no Spaniard would have dreamt of picking a fig at any time but breakfast.

Tapas time began several hours later, when the streets became redolent of deep-fried squid and roasting chorizo. *Los amigos* could usually be found in the Fonda or any of the many taverns tucked away in unlikely, and even unimaginable places, on the winding alleys and staircases of the village. And if you couldn't find the person you wanted, you just had to ask *Maria Platillo Volante* and she either told you immediately, or made it her business to inform the interested party where you were, so that one way or the other you were with him in less time than it takes, nowadays, to send and receive an e-mail.

Maria was the town peanut-vendor. In her black dress and slippers she roamed the bars with a broad basket over her arm, supplying the drinkers with *avellanas*, as the villagers wrongly called them, confusing peanuts with hazelnuts. She got her strange nickname ("Mary the Flying Saucer", by which she is known until today, even though the reason has been largely forgotten) because she was constantly "orbiting" around the town, like the UFO's and sputniks which were then all the rage. Maria's life had been "ruined" by a scoundrel who left her with five illegitimate children to marry someone else, and she lived with her scrawny, anemic brood in a cellar on the Calle de Marquesas, sustaining them all on her peanut sales, which literally amounted to what we would call "peanuts".

Lilo immediately made her our friend, for Maria was, like Lilo, a lady with great spiritual qualities, as one could see from her lovely, soulful dark eyes. We would sometimes give her a few hours of work making our lunch, and I can see her in my mind's eye now, smiling sadly as she stirs her delicious *revuelto* of eggplants and potatoes in garlic and olive oil, in the long-handled iron pan sizzling on the coals in the primitive kitchen.

Sometimes I would get up early and walk out of the village with Cristobal, while he delivered the bread to the *cortijos*. He wore a grey cotton waistcoat and cap and broad canvas trousers, and led a mule laden with hemp-woven *cerrones*, saddle bags, full of big loaves of bread. On the way he would sing the chants we all loved, the *caña*, which was the wagoneer's song, and the *serrana*, the "mountain girl's" song. He did not have Manolo's magical subtlety, but it was wonderful to hear, along the white roads in the fresh mountain air. When "breakfast" time came (they only drank coffee or anisette upon rising, and had their real breakfast in mid-morning) we would stop in the shade of an almond tree to share a *canto de pan y aceite*. He would take out his curved jack-knife and cut a big piece from the side of one of the round loaves. Then he carved a wedge of dough from the interior and filled the hole with thick, green olive oil from a small bottle he carried in his pouch, with the cork attached to the neck by a string. He replaced the wedge, and when the oil had been properly absorbed, broke it in two. This was eaten with a cucumber which we peeled and held in one hand like a banana, and washed down with water from his clay *pipote*, a jug with a thin spout like a tea-pot, which he filled at a nearby fountain and then held in the air so that the water poured in a stream into his open mouth.

Although we seemed very strange to them - *una alemana* with a crew-cut and *un inglés* with hair which for those pre-hippie years was very long - it never occurred to anyone to ask if, for example, we were married. We came from a different world, where their laws did not apply. All they knew was that we were in their village - the first foreigners they had ever seen - and that we liked it and came back often, and because of this we were welcome in every home, from the poorest hovel to our *señorito* Don Curro's manor, the Torre del Sol, west of town.

That was where I got the sunburn, sitting by his swimming pool, the only one in Montefrio. He had built it for the tourist girls he picked up in Torremolinos, where his parents had a villa, but he never bathed in it himself, since in his traditional way of thinking, the proper place for a man of quality was the *sombra*, the shade - direct exposure to the sun and elements was a curse inflicted on field labourers and fishermen only. And the painful memory I have of his pool would seem to confirm his position. When Lilo and I were bathing in it one afternoon, I became absorbed in the reading of Don Quijote, and had covered my back with a shirt but forgotten about my legs, which were hanging in the water. By the time we got home that evening I was howling with pain, and spent the next two weeks in bed, with my skin bright red from the knees up. This caused some wonderment in the town, since it was the first case of sunburn they had ever witnessed - as I have said, only the *cortijeros* exposed themselves to the elements, and they were like well-tanned leather. The pain became so unbearable that Lilo had to call in the local *practicante*, Don Juan, who back then wore a black, Franco-style moustache, to inject me with a sleeping potion. She was out when he arrived, and I remember seeing him down the stairs after the shot and then barely making it back up to the bed before being struck completely unconscious. In those days the *médico* was a proud figure who rarely left his office and charged dearly for his services, so these para-physicians or male nurses, served as the de facto physicians for most of the community. Today, at the end of the millennium, Don Juan, long since retired, is said to have delivered most of the villagers over the age of 40.

But the one I wanted to be with all the time was Manolo, Manolo the artist - perhaps the only one I ever met who really deserved the name. In fact he was a poet, a singing poet, because, like all real poets, he was incapable of uttering a word which was not poetry, even though he never wrote a line. Flamenco singers do not speak of singing a particular verse, but of "saying" it, because, in the medieval tradition, they are singing poets, who declaim their tales, their philosophical maxims, and Manolo was a poet in the medieval tradition.

97

Together we wandered, we talked, and whenever the urge seized him, he sang. I heard him sing among his olive trees on the hillside called Vaciacámaras, and in the ruins of the great 16th century church on the cliff, before the hole in the roof - caused by the celebrated lightning bolt of 1767 - was repaired. I heard him sing among the stalactites of the prehistoric caves called Las Peñas de los Gitanos, and I heard him sing on the Calvary Hill overlooking the village, where I took an eerie photograph of him with his arms raised and the great vein standing out on his forehead, a photograph which I had forgotten until it re-appeared 20 years later in a trunk I had left in Yves' cellar in Paris.

In September there was a livestock fair which brought hundreds, or perhaps even thousands of farmers, each with his waistcoat and boots and walking stick, *callao*, hanging over his arm, to buy and sell horses, mules and donkeys. The two gypsy brothers, Melchor and José, who were horse dealers by trade, invited me to get up on a mare they had - my first ride bareback - which promptly began to run across the field, with me hanging on to the mane, until a man in the crowd got hold of its dangling bridle. Their father was an imposing fellow with great moustaches called Guillermo, whom I always thought of as the King of the Gypsies. Like all gypsy patriarchs, he had total authority over his children, even when they were grown men themselves. Once, while conversing in the plaza, Melchor - who then was about 25 and had several children of his own - said something which apparently displeased his father, and without saying a word he sharply slapped his face. To my amazement, Melchor acquiesced, hanging his head in shame.

But that did not mean that they were not proud - when Melchor admired a bright yellow knitted tie I had brought from New York, and which I was rather tired of (we were all very dapper then), I said that I would give it to him. The next time we met, in the plaza among a group of other gypsies, I took it out of my jacket pocket and offered it to him, but he frowned and hurriedly motioned me to put it back. "Later", he whispered, "when we're alone".

As for my life with Lilo, it was too soon for the troubles to begin, but there was an advance signal, in the comic form of a tossed flower pot. My dear friend Anthony came from New York to spend a few weeks with us, and one night, after he and I had been up late talking in the kitchen, thoughtlessly leaving Lilo upstairs as young people will do, we decided to go out for a walk. But as soon as we closed the door behind us and stepped into the street, there was a great explosion, with earth and leaves flying everywhere. We looked up at the balcony of the bedroom. Lilo was no longer there, nor was the large flowerpot of geraniums... The problem was that Lilo had always had me to herself, and I had adjusted my outpourings to her serious, German way of reasoning. When she heard me chattering away freely in my naturally irreverent Anglo-Saxon vein, she didn't like it. Later on, when she met my mother in Paris, she bitterly, and jealously denounced it as "decadent and devilish".

But Anthony went away, carrying a pitchfork made from a single tree into the tiny aircraft on the Granada airfield, because it wouldn´t fit in the luggage compartment, and for a short while more, all was harmony and understanding. Such are the perils of being a cultural chameleon - one's diversity can be misconstrued as duplicity. But before we left for decadent, devilish Paris, at the end of the summer, we did something which, as an American would say, was right up her Wagnerian alley (and Lilo's surname was in fact Wagner): we spent three nights sleeping in a tomb.

Several miles east of Montefrio lies the vast archaeological site known as Las Peñas de los Gitanos - The Cliffs of the Gypsies. We decided to get closer to the mysteries of this lovely spot by sleeping in one of the Copper Age "dolmens", or megalithic tombs, which litter the floor of the great canyon. Thus one fine day in August we set out from Montefrio, with the hired help of El Gordo and his donkey, laden with our groceries and a few of Manolo's sheepskins to sleep on. When the villagers learned where we were going they murmured in awe, "¡Van a dormir con los muertos!".

We were comfortable enough, just fitting into the floor of the tomb, with our branches and leaves and the fluffy *zaleas*, and Cristobal came out every day with his mule to bring us fresh bread and see how we were getting along. We saw no Copper Age spirits, or any Bronze Age ones either, but we did get a portentous glimpse of the shape of things to come. The first space satellites had just been launched by the Russians and then the Americans, and it was lying out one night under the summer sky on the great slab of rock which covered the tomb that we saw one for the first time. We could only tell it apart from the stars because it was moving, on an even but uncharted course, towards the future - like us.

Even before I first set foot in Montefrio, Manolo was already famous enough for the fledgling Spanish television company to want to film him singing in his butcher shop. In 1957 a crew with a cameraman came, causing great excitement among the villagers, since television was something they had only heard about then, their town being far from the nearest transmitters.

I have taken a few images from this short film which show the great man behind his counter, wearing an unusually clean white shirt and apron for the occasion. First he listens to the guitar beginning the sacred *siguiriyas*, like an old lion waiting for his prey to come near. Then he catches the scent and pricks up his ears, freezing for a moment until he gives out a triumphant roar that, before going in for the kill, subsides into a blood-curdling snarl...

A flamenco singer is like an opera singer – if he (or she) doesn't have *la presencia*, it doesn't work!And compared to most of his fellow *cantaores*, Manolo had the right looks...

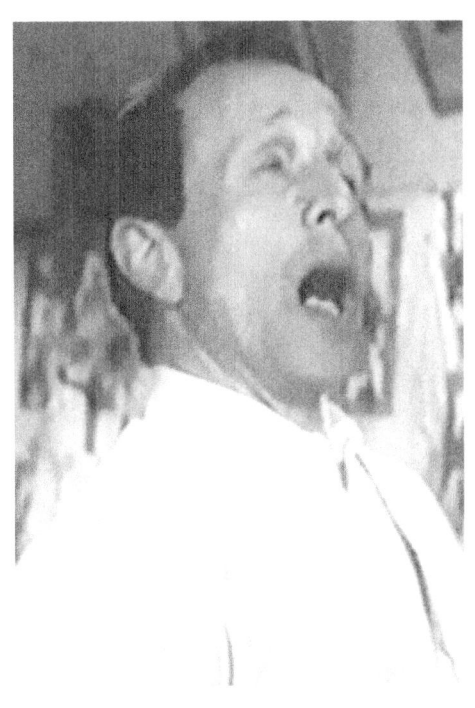

The Englishman Goes Away

I would be straying from my subject if I were to describe that first school year in Paris which came between our two summers in Montefrio. Suffice it to say that the time between September 1961 and July 1962 was full of exciting new things, and people, which had the effect of driving a wedge between me and my strong-willed companion. The recurrent presence of my vivacious young mother, herself very much "on the road", didn't help matters, either.

Just before we left for Spain, at the end of the school year, a girl Lilo had studied painting with in Munich turned up at our servant's room under the rooftop of a house in the 17th arrondissement. She seemed alienated, as they said then, and lonely, was very pretty in the wholesome German way, and my reaction was that of any bored young rooster upon finding a comely new hen in his nest. I went out of my way to be amusing and accommodating, Lilo was pleased to lecture Elke about art and what-not, and the girl almost naturally decided to come along with us to Spain for the summer.

These fortuitious romances went very fast back then, and the Puerta del Sol had not even pulled out of Austerlitz Station before Elke and I were getting discreetly entwined in the crowded, murky compartments. The combination of the summer heat and our extreme youth had us inflamed, and by the time we got to Madrid, Lilo was having a hard time ignoring it . We memorably managed to get lost in the Forest of Aranjuez for several hours, leaving her with a Spanish friend of mine to search for us along the paths. It was therefore hardly surprising, we all being what we were, that almost as soon as we got to Montefrio things reached a literally violent climax.

We stayed the first night in the Fonda until the house was readied for us, and after dinner I took Elke for a walk in the olive groves, and in case you didn't know, the expression "to go for a walk in the olive groves" has a special significance in these parts. I can still see her milky white body in the moonlight, half-reclining on a slope near the great stone crucifix known as Cruz Gorda, which blesses travellers taking the old road to Granada. When I got back to the room in the early hours, Lilo expressed her rage by falling to her knees in front of me and beating her head on the tile floor, several times over and without saying a word. I was horrified, but, in my pragmatic Anglo-Saxon way, couldn't help feeling relieved that it was not my head.

In spite of this dramatic, but useless gesture, an external propriety was maintained and Lilo seemed to decide to let things run their course. After all, back in Schwabing, Munich's bohemian quarter where she had lived, such situations were quite common. A month followed in which we did the same things we had done the summer before, except that when night came I waited for Lilo to pretend to fall asleep before joining Elke on her straw-filled mattress down the corridor. I would be back before dawn, and the two women spent the day amiably, or at least politely, painting and cooking together. Since they spoke in German I don't know exactly what they were saying, but was glad to take note that it did not seem to be about me!

The only other memory I distinctly have of that summer, less idyllic than the previous one, was the flamenco party in the *cortijo*. Manolo and I arranged with the gypsies to have a party in a farmhouse on the outskirts of the village, and we all set off in the night with a big straw-covered jug of wine and a basket of things to munch on. The fiesta was going full swing, with myself and the Munich milk-maid doing a joyous number in the light of the oil lamp, when suddenly, as if by magic, all the gypsies disappeared into the darkness. When we went out on the porch to see what had happened, we saw the silhouettes of two Civil Guardsmen approaching in the moonlight, with their gleaming winged hats and rifles slung over their shoulders. Although the traditional enemies of the gypsies ruined our party (because we had failed to obtain the written authorization which was necessary, under Franco, to hold an assembly of over 20 persons), I was always thrilled when the images of Lorca's poetry seemed to step, as they often did then, out of the pages of the *Romancero Gitano*.

Then one morning, I returned to our bedroom and found Lilo gone, with a note under the alarm clock which had been set in time to catch the seven o'clock *correo* to Granada. She said she was going to Ibiza to find a house for her parents and sister to spend the summer holidays, and that if I wanted to follow...

I was hardly shocked after all the liberties I had taken, but it all seemed suddenly dull and uninteresting with just me and Elke - who, you will appreciate, was no *ersatz* for Fraulein Wagner - alone in the big house, and a few days later I decided to send her back to Germany. There was a sad parting at the Granada railway station, as she went north and I took the train to Valencia. Lilo was waiting for me as the boat drew up to the pier in Ibiza, marching back and forth with a defiant expression on her face. But we were soon like fingers of the same hand, once more.

We had been in Ibiza the summer before, to visit another Munich friend of Lilo's, a large, restless creature who looked like Cleopatra just after getting out of bed, and who, by the time we got there, had actually been there, in bed that is, with half the men on the island and moved out to Formentera, where we found her living in temporary monogamy with a Dane, in a tiny cement box on a stony field in the middle of nowhere. The two islands were well on their way to becoming the meeting place for all the misfits of Europe, and Formentera was the last frontier.

This year, though, we stayed put under the auspices of Mutti and Fatti in their beach cottage in Santa Eulalia. Across the inlet the surveyors were marking out the site for the island's first modern hotel, and the few foreigners stayed in makeshift cement houses thrown together along the shore. In the one in front of us, the Spanish caretaker spent much of the day hoisting buckets of water onto the roof to fill the holding tank which enabled his guests to have showers when they came from the beach. I never shared the idyllic feelings which some people have about Ibiza, and many years later - as you will see a few pages on - my indifference turned into downright aversion. So I will describe the most memorable thing which happened to us there, and get back to Montefrio.

This, however, requires me to move backwards first. When we got to Paris the previous autumn, we stayed in a walk-up student's hotel on the Carrefour de l'Odéon, administered by two old concierges, unmarried sisters. Like many such Frenchwomen in those Gaullist times, they were unnecessarily nasty and constantly complained about "Mademoiselle Wagner's" loud boots clattering on the wooden staircase, and my own attempts to play *Fandangillos de Huelva* on the guitar. When we left the Nouvel Hotel for the *chambre de bonne* on the Rue Rennequin, we put these two shrews out of our minds forever, as you can imagine.

Now, in Ibiza - 10 months later - we were riding our rental bikes one morning down one of the island's inland roads, crossing a long stretch of arid fields, divided by stone walls and the occasional gnarled almond tree - when, under the blazing sun, we saw, shimmering in the distance, two stooped female silhouettes heading towards us. As we drew closer, we saw that they were not native *ibicencas*, and that they were both staring at us as if we were a divine apparition. When they began to babble excitedly in French, "*Mademoiselle Wagner! Monsieur Bohme!*" we realized that they were the two concierges from Paris. It seemed they had a cousin who stayed in Ibiza during the summer whom they had come to visit, but what was most extraordinary was that, due to the highly unlikely circumstances and (in their minds) the distance from civilization, they now saw us as their long-lost daughter and son. It was hardly the moment to remind them of how horrible they had been to us when we were their tenants, so, feeling rather sorry for the old fools, we pretended to be pleased...

But our last month together in Spain - and, in fact, the second from last of all of our months together - was truly idyllic, in a setting of perfect, undefiled beauty. We had heard the year before of a cluster of mountain villages on the southern flanks of the Sierra Nevada, called the Alpujarra, and decided to spend a month there before returning to France. It was in Capileira's only, primitive *pensión* that Lilo cut my long hair, so that the next day the villagers who saw us thought, and even said aloud, that the little man had exchanged his large female companion for a large male one with a haircut just like his.

We rented the top floor of an ancient house overhanging the deep river valley, from two old farmers, for 25 pesetas per day, today the cost of a local phone call. The houses of the Alpujarra were originally built by the Moors in the style native to the Altas Mountains: heavy horizontal beams covered with large sheets of natural slate and sealed with a fine waterproof clay, making each roof a terrace where the family can sit among the rows of drying tomatoes and lumpy white chimneys, overlooking all the other flat roofs which cling, like an undulating staircase, to the mountainside.

We brought water up in a jug from the fountain, cooked on a fire of sticks, and used a chamber pot the contents of which the old folks told us could be thrown off the edge of the terrace into the trees. Like the villagers, we lived on a stew made of *garbanzos*, dried peppers and tomatoes, with whatever greens Antonio brought back from his huerta, except each Friday when a tiny donkey came up from the city of Orgija, at the foot of the mountain, loaded with fresh fish. Everyone came out with saucepans to buy half a kilo as the donkey passed, and soon the whole village smelled deliciously of frying *boquerones*. It was the weekly gastronomical treat.

We spent the days as usual, me typing out a novel on my portable typewriter, and Lilo painting portraits of the neighbours. In the afternoons we roamed the paths among the terraced orchards, always green with the waters of the melting snows. When a storm blew up from below, it would engulf one tiny white village after the other in its course, until Capileira seemed to be alone at the top of the world. In fact, that is what the Arabized Roman name means: the capillary or "hairy" top of the head. On very clear days, we could see ships steaming towards Gibraltar, far below on a strip of pastel blue sea.

As long as Lilo and I remained in this monastic environment, everything seemed like it might go on forever. But a few weeks later we were back in the belly of the beast, pre-1968 Paris, among others of our own mind and generation, surrounded by agitation, newness and an endless range of fascinating options - and fellow travellers - to choose from. There followed a breathless school year in Paris without Lilo (or, rather, fleeing from Lilo), a summer on the loose far from Spain, and then, at the end of 1963, I packed my duffle bags to return to the Americas, seemingly forever. By the time a conjuncture of chance, curiosity and world-weariness brought me to Montefrio again, I was a man of 41 years.

*These pictures of a village reminiscent of Montefrio as it was then
are from the Civil War film "The Spanish Earth"*

Visitor from the Past

Up to the age of 40, it had always been my philosophy that it was best never to stop still or even look back. It was the code of the footloose adventurer. But upon reaching mid-life, the feeling that I had already seen quite a bit led me to start doing just those two things. In fact, I began to want something I had never really had: my own home, but less in the sense of "house" than "place".

I returned to Europe, from the West Indies, in 1981, and spent the first two years in France. I had gone there hoping to continue with my arts and crafts business on the Cote d'Azur but, for purely economic reasons, ended up becoming a translator in Paris instead. Then I unexpectedly received a modest but regular monthly sum of money which made it possible to live without working for quite a few years, but not in Paris. I asked my benefactor - who knew me well - where I should go and the answer was "Spain". So I went to have a look, it being understood that Spain for me meant this particular corner of it.

When, that damp spring morning, I got on the bus at the El Tocón railway station - fifth stop on the Granada-Algeciras line - it had been almost 21 years that I left Montefrio for the last time. A few letters had been exchanged after my departure, because Lilo had melodramatically written to Maria the peanut peddler that "Lorenzo's heart is dead", and the naïve lady went about announcing my biological death, until a letter commissioned by Manolo reached me in Paris asking for a confirmation. I recognised my ex-girlfriend's *sturm und drang* and wrote back explaining that all she meant was that I was a heartless bastard for having left her. But after that, I relegated Montefrio to the magical past, and all contact was lost. There were so many other things, and places, that vied for my attention, then!

Manolo was the person I most wanted to see but, since he would now be 70, it was my turn to feel worried, as the bus began to climb north through the pine forests. I turned to the elderly farmer sitting next to me, in his grey cotton suit and straw hat, and asked nervously if Manuel Avila was still alive. His answer itself was a spiritual return to Montefrio: *"¡Si lo está"*, he assured me enthusiastically, *"y muy buena persona es!"* - Yes, and a fine fellow he is too. To have just answered straightforwardly "Yes, he is alive" without adding a rhetorical word of praise might give the impression that he wouldn't regret it if Manolo were dead.

Having read and heard so much about how Spain had changed since the sixties, I was satisfied to see that although Montefrio had changed too, it had done so much less than the other places I had seen on my journey south from Madrid. There were the same well-groomed olive groves and spectacular approach, as the castle and village seem to rise up from the valley below, and the odd-shaped plaza was still odd-shaped, although the whitewashed fronts of the buildings, once warped and lumpy, had almost all been rebuilt and straightened out. It was like seeing an old man who had just been fitted with a set of disturbingly perfect false teeth.

One thing struck me immediately: the large black wooden cross which had been affixed to the front of the great round church, along with the list of names of right-wing Civil War victims "vilely murdered by the Marxists", had been removed. I might not have remembered it if it were not for the fact that the cross had left a ghost-like, pale silhouette on the ochre-coloured stone. In fact, just a few days before, the villagers had voted in a Communist mayor, whose first act was to remove Franco's intolerable war memorial. But since the decision of the *Consejo* had only called for the removal of the crucifix, the workers were unable to sand or grind away the mark it had left - which, to my mind, created a much more powerful effect than the cross itself.

The house we had lived in still stood in 1983, with the same door which we had unlocked with the big key we were given by the owner in Cordoba. Manolo no longer lived in the same house nearby, but the woman there – who immediately recognized me, although not I her, because she said she had been our cleaning woman - told me he would not be found in his current house either, but at his sister's on the Calle Alta, above his nephew's shoe shop. A little boy was instructed to take me there. A few minutes later I stood in a somber room lined with shoe boxes, where a plump, balding man excitedly said he remembered me from when he was 10 years old, before rushing upstairs to call his uncle.

Manolo was not so enchanted, and with good reason - I had never once written in all that time. He glanced at me unsmilingly and sat down without saying a word. For a moment I wretchedly thought he was going to tell me to go to hell, but after a while he grunted *"Pensé que te habían matao"* - I thought they had killed you. I recognized this as another one of those set phrases which they use to neutralize potentially embarrassing situations and began to apologize, but he motioned me to stop. He had rapped my knuckles for being such a rascal, but he knew he would have done just the same if he had gone away, and what I had been up to for the past 20 years didn't interest him anyway. In fact, he immediately made it clear that there were only two subjects which he felt could possibly interest anyone: flamenco singing, and his ailments, and as soon as he had taken full stock of my presence, he began lecturing me on both of them, a bit of one and then a bit of the other.

He looked very dignified in his retirement clothes, dark suit with prize-winning gold guitar-shaped pin in the lapel and neatly trimmed grey-white hair. He told me that he had been recently installed with a pace-maker (the villagers joked about it, saying he "had a guitar in his breast") and suffered from a host of afflictions which made it totally impossible for him to sing - in spite of which he sang, in short bursts, all day long. In fact, Manolo had become such a hypochondriac that when I told him so one day, he pounced avidly on what he thought was a new pathological condition and shouted, "You're right, I've got that too!", until I explained what it meant and his triumph turned to bitter indignation.

Long-suffering Maria was in Barcelona taking care of their two sons, who worked in a factory, and I was told that they now officially resided there. But since Manolo couldn't stand Barcelona, he in fact spent half of his time back in the village, sleeping in the empty house on the Calle Baja but spending the day at his sister's, above the shoe shop on the Calle Alta. For the tormented artist, Montefrio was the lesser of two evils: when I imprudently asked him if he was "happier" in Montefrio or Barcelona, hoping he would say Montefrio, he looked at me indignantly and snarled, *"¡No estoy bien en ninguna parte!"* - I'm not happy anywhere! I knew what he meant. One has to live somewhere on the face of the earth, and for Manolo - as well as for me, it soon proved - Montefrio was it.

But the one who made me decide to return to stay was not Manolo but kind, innocent, brotherly Cristobal, the *panadero* who delivered the bread to the farms. Early the next morning I was sitting on the toilet in the Fonda, where I had taken a room for the night, which I recognized as the same room No. 5 where Lilo had beaten her head on the tiled floor, when the staircase leading up from the street reverberated with a series of great shouts. Someone had told the good man I was back, and he had raced over from the bakery. He still looked just like one of his rough loaves of bread, except with a little more flour sprinkled on top and more yeast in the dough. I was hugged, stroked, shouted at, hugged again and, within minutes, bundled into the already ancient van in which he now delivered his bread to the farms.

Off we bounced down the dirt roads. The mule had been sent to pasture many years ago, and the van made too much noise for him to sing as we went along, but not to talk, or rather shout. I was confronted with the big question which everyone was asking of me, "Where is Lilo?", since, to my dismay, they had all been fondly remembering us as an inseparable unit. I awkwardly explained that I had not seen her since a few months after leaving Montefrio, in other words, since almost as long as I had not seen them. The next question was an incredulous "Why?", and all I could do was mumble about life taking us on different paths, which the women took very poorly. In Montefrio you may treat your wife as badly as you wish, but you never leave her.

However, I soon devised an answer for the men, which went down quite well, explaining that I was very young then and "still longed to meet many other women".

Maria Platillo Volante, my old friend told me, had also moved to Barcelona, where her five children, transformed by the industrial boom from useless lumpen into essential manpower, had found work in the factories and were able to look after her in her old age. She returned once a year, I was told, in a tiny SEAT 600 jelly-bean to see her relatives and buy olive oil and garbanzos to take back to her Catalonian tenement flat. Melchor the gypsy worked in a brewery in Barcelona operating the machine which put the labels on the cans, and was "fat and very well". His brother José had moved to a nearby town, where he still sold horses. I would soon be embraced and interrogated by them all...

It was when Cristobal stopped to attend to some almond trees of his that I realized what I would do. He was grafting "sweet almond" shoots onto a tree which he said was "bitter", when I saw across the ravine a woman with a straw hat washing clothes under a fig tree, in front of a crooked white house. Down below by the creek a boy was calling up to his mother, in the perfect silence of the cactus and olive trees. I said to Cristobal, "I want to live in a house like that".

Two months later I was back in my grey Fiat van with its Alpes-Maritimes licence plates, loaded with everything I owned, including an electric typewriter and a gas-powered camping fridge newly purchased at La Samaritaine. After a few days of driving about in the bread truck, with Cristobal pointing first to one uninhabited cortijo and then to another, I chose an old mule-drivers' tavern on the road between Algarinejo and Montefrio, because it had a sweeping view of the Milanos Valley. There, I settled down to finish writing my life story, the still unfinished manuscript of which I later, half on purpose, managed to lose. My amorous ventures were more consequential, if not precisely more successful than my literary ones, and within a month of my arrival I had fallen in love with a problematic young woman from a nearby town, whose destiny I believed for a while to be entwined with mine. To the point that I began to look for a cortijo to buy, because, having just been expelled from university because of insufficient attendance, she felt that she could make a go of a business which was then the rage, a "farm school", where city children were indoctrinated to the joys of rural living over the weekend. I wrote the story of my adventures with Rocio but mislaid it, too, perhaps for the better. Suffice it to say that after she and her whimsical *granja escuela* had gone by the board, what remained was something totally new for me: the determination to have a house of my own.

It happened at the livestock fair of June, 1985. I was inspecting a rather puny mare, which a local man called Yo-Yo wanted urgently to sell me. I explained that I couldn't buy a horse because I didn't have a cortijo to keep it in. Yo-Yo, with an entrepreneurial gleam in his eye, asked what sort of house I was looking for. Small plot of land, good roof, beautiful views, low price... a moment later I was on the back of his motorbike, bumping down another *carril*. There it stood, like a chalk-white balcony overlooking the Sierra de Parapanda and the plain of Granada, nestling among oak and almond and fig trees. My self-appointed real estate agent said it was owned by five brothers, all of whom had moved to Barcelona except one, who was ready to part with it for a price I could afford. The next day the house was mine - although I never did buy the mare.

No Boat from Valencia

It would be two weeks before the workers could begin remodelling my recently acquired cortijo, and what with the fine spring weather, I decided that the time had finally come to visit Lilo. Over the 20-odd years since we last stood face to face in the fresco room of the École des Beaux Arts in Paris, I had never lost contact with her entirely. Every time she had an exhibit in Ibiza, where she had been living ever since, she sent a poster to my father's address, with a message written on the back in her big, square handwriting, and from Canada it was forwarded to me in Brazil or Haiti or wherever I was. She knew I was back in Europe, and had even written inviting me to stay with her in her brother's villa, where she was running, in the warmer months, a sort of ashram or cultural centre, with courses in Zen Buddhism, vegetarian cooking, and so forth.

Not being much inclined towards that sort of thing, and feeling some dismay that the fiercely independent Lilo could have finally cast her lot with what I sometimes describe as "the wilted flower generation", I stayed away. Also, I didn't fully trust her mellow, detached tone, and feared being lured into a trap full of recriminations and, even, renewed amorous overtures. But, I hoped, a surprise visit in the summer would catch her off guard and - what with the other people in the house - with her hands tied, so to speak. In any case, she had no phone, and I made my decision one day and left the next.

Planes were fully booked so I had to go by the ferry. I took the bus to Valencia, as in the old days, but when I got to the wharf was informed that the boat now left from Denia, down the coast. A streamlined white ocean cruiser as big as an office building was waiting by the jetty, with the choppy Mediterranean behind it, announcing the new order of things: Ibiza, which I had visited in the early 60's when it

111

was a meeting place for down-and-out bohemians (of which Lilo was one of the last hangers-on), and to which one acceded on a rusty tramp, was now big business.

So I was braced for the worst. Montefrio and Ibiza belonged to the same national territory, but otherwise they were in different galaxies. The boat didn't even dock at the charming port anymore, but put me and the horde of young sightseers off on the other side of the island, where everything was conveniently laid out, like Florida. A sleek taxi cab swept me up an asphalt road like a black carpet and in a few minutes let me off at the foot of the hill on which stood Lilo's village, Balafi. It was almost dusk but I could recognise, jutting up from the small mound of peasant houses, the two Moorish watchtowers which she and I had discovered in wonderment on our rented bikes in the summer of 1962, and one of which, according to her letters, had been her home almost ever since.

There was a restaurant on the corner, and before setting out on the path which led to the village, I went in to ask about her, thinking that she might even be there, having her dinner. A Spanish man with a black beard was standing alone at the bar, but when I asked him if he knew Lilo Wagner, he stared at me blankly and said *"Está muerta"*. In the next few hundred seconds I had learned from him and the barman that, 11 days before, she had thrown herself into the well of her brother's villa. The barman, who was also the owner and half-drunk, said that Lilo was a very nice person but crazy, and that she would sometimes come down from her tower in the village and kneel in front of him, as if he were a prophet. I imagined the loneliness which had driven her to such self-humiliation.

In my confusion and horror, and it being night with, suddenly, nowhere to stay, I shouldered my satchel and set out on foot to Santa Eulalia on the coast, where, I thought, at least there would be lights, life, and, perhaps, people who had never known Lilo. It was longer than I remembered, and I stumbled as much because of the darkness as the stampede of thoughts in my mind.

But it's a small island, and I was soon having dinner in a tastefully decorated seafood restaurant, of which the owner and customers were all well-tanned and well-built Germans. I slept in a hotel across the road from a butcher shop which, in so far as I could understand from the sign above the door, made authentic bratwurst and leberwurst. Just as they said, Ibiza had become a German island in the Mediterranean, and I imagined how Lilo must have hated seeing it taken over by those she always loathingly called "the pigs". In the morning I went back to Balafi to find out what I could.

When I look over all I have written about Lilo Wagner, I wonder for a moment how I could ever got involved with her at all, what with her outlandish behaviour and violent nature, of which her suicide at age 45 was the final and (many of her friends opine) logical consequence. But, as I walked up the path to Balafi in the morning sunlight, leaving the car I had rented on the road, I was reminded of the fine side of Lilo, her adoration of this same land which she had discovered in the Aegean and the frescoes of Giotto, the delicately twisted almond trees of which each tiny leaf was like a miniature painting, the web of rough stone walls dividing ochre-coloured patches of land, each of which somehow gave sustenance to a goat and a sprinkling of bright red poppies. It was the Mediterranean which I had read of as a child in the famous book about Capri, The Story of San Michele, with its world of free-flying thought, luminous conversation and open-hearted friendship, which Lilo and I had once idealistically shared.

In the hamlet, which is nothing more than a cluster of rough white houses scattered along a few paths, I found three women working in a garden, in black dresses and straw hats, and asked them which of the two squat, conical towers Lilo had lived in. They fell silent and one of them pointed to the one closest to us. The door was padlocked but, looking over the gate, I could see the white dome-covered well where she had drawn her water, the ramshackle wooden terrace where she had taken the sun, the rough flagstones of the courtyard which she had crossed to step out into the whitewashed alley. I went back and spoke to the women, who answered in *ibizenco*. One of them said they had all thought highly of Lilo - *estimava molt* - and I explained that I was a very old friend of hers who had come to visit her, and had just been told she had died.

I asked them to pick me some flowers to put on her grave in the cemetery at the entrance to the village, and, as they instructed, went to the nearby grocery store to get the key. Again, when I mentioned Lilo's name to the storekeeper, her face clouded over. She had known her for many years, and when her daughter was sick Lilo had come to visit her every day. Among the poor, simple people, Lilo's noble side had always shone. It was only her own kind that brought out the rage.

I walked to the long white wall broken only by a sun-bleached wooden door in which the ancient key turned and - just as the woman said - immediately to the right saw a wooden cross with two metal initials fixed to it, "LW". The grave was covered with flowers which had already gone brown in the sun, and to which I added my few fresh ones.

In the afternoon, I went back to take photographs of Lilo's tower, and passing in front of its twin, noticed several oil paintings drying in the sun. Another ivory tower, I thought. Here, I would learn more.

I stepped through the open door into an artist's studio. Everything resembled my mother's own interiors: the indirect sunlight, the careful disorder, the pastel-coloured flowers, the discreetly abstract paintings. Even the woman who appeared in answer to my call was, curiously, the image of my mother too, when she was a handsome blonde woman roaming the world with her crates of canvases and teenage son.

"So, you are Lawrence", she said, sitting in front me. "Every winter I told her, 'Come back to Munich with me' - you know how cold and miserable it gets here in the winter, and she had no proper heating, just the *brasero*, she didn't even have electricity - but she would always say, 'No, not this winter, this winter Lawrence will come'". I imagined the rainy months in the primitive tower, going blind reading by the oil lamp and trying to play Bach on the flute - it was Lilo's quest for self-chastisement, atoning for all of our sins.

"It was the house that ruined her. Before, she was alright, when she just had the tower. Oh, she was crazy of course - her family refused to send her any more money and she tried to get jobs whitewashing walls and gardening, but it was barely enough to survive. But she had her cats and her paintings, and we all loved to talk to her, she was so funny and kind. It was Can Micaeleta that killed her, all those terrible people that came, from all over the world, she thought they were going to help her do something wonderful and beautiful but they only wanted to use her."

Apparently, her brother in Germany gave her the run of the house in exchange for taking care of it, and she had decided to try to make a little money and Improve Mankind in the process by creating the art-and-philosophy course. But it proved to be a disaster - the fliers she sent out mostly drew freeloaders, and some of them spent the summer there "studying", and then said they couldn't pay. One Swedish girl was not only unable to pay, but tried to raise the money to fly back to Sweden by spreading all her tattered belongings on the terrace and waiting, saddhu-like with her legs crossed, for people to buy them... Lilo, horrified, gave her the money she needed out of her own pocket and drove her to the airport.

I asked how she had come to throw herself in the well. "She would go crazy with them all there, like helpless children waiting for her to cook and do things for them. One day the water stopped coming out of the taps and Lilo thought that the pump had broken down, but in fact the well had run completely dry because they had been using so much water. She went to the well-house with a few others to see if they could do something, the pump worked but still there was no water, and she suddenly became hysterical and got up on the edge and jumped in. I got there a few hours after the police removed her. An Englishman who had just arrived on the island and who had seen her jump was still wandering around the house in a daze, mumbling to himself...".

What a way to begin your summer course in transcendental meditation, I thought. But for a long time after that I, too, would find myself mumbling the words of the barman of Es Pins, *"treinta metros sin agua"*.

"I don't know how Lilo knew so many attractive men", she said looking at me, "at her funeral I was amazed by all the impressive, distinguished men, journalists and professors, who came from Madrid, from Barcelona, even from Germany, to bury her". It was simple, I explained: other women used their beauty and charm to attract men, and Lilo used her native wit and brains. But they never loved her, they just wanted to be her friend, as I had.

She wanted to show me Can Micaeleta before it got dark, because they had cut off the electricity. We drove to a pine forest, a padlocked gate, a dirt road, a large, handsome white house standing silently in the dusk, and, on the rambling, weed-covered grounds, the well, made of unfinished cinder blocks...

We walked through the pine trees, past a few dozen daffodils growing all on their own, as if they were wild, on the beaten earth. Somehow, they looked like people or friends that you could talk to. My guide shook her head and said, "Who will take care of her lovely garden now?". I imagined the proper, well-protected flower beds which would take their place, as soon as her brother in Frankfurt found a buyer. A cat ran across our path; she shrugged and said that there was a whole community of them.

The electricity had been shut off so we had to take the boxes of papers close to the window. There was a photo of Lilo, emaciated and somehow shrunken, laughing clownishly, but otherwise unrecognisable to me, and when I saw it I agreed with what the woman had said earlier, that it was just as well that I had not had to face her in life. The paintings and drawings had, I was told, become progressively less crafted and representative, ending in shapeless scraps of line and colour, like the botched attempts of a prehistoric cave artist. I chose an elaborately shaded pen-and-ink of a gnarled root, dated 1965, and put it in my satchel as a memento of the woman who made me realize I could draw.

On the way out she waved her hand at the wall of book shelves, filled almost to the ceiling with volumes in German, English, French, Spanish, on art, religion, philosophy, and I'll never forget the good woman's words: "So much knowledge, but she couldn't learn how to live!".

Outside, she seemed to want to turn her back on failure and death and smiled at me like a sister, as if the fact that we had both been loved by Lilo had created a bond between us. "You don't have to go back tomorrow, you know, you can stay for a few days", she said, almost beseechingly.

But suddenly, all I wanted was to be in Granada, in the student house where Rocio was living that spring near the Puerta de Elvira, the one with the pretty yellow weeds growing on the roof.

Seven Olive Trees

I gave the house a name because it didn't really have one of its own - the local people simply referred to it as *la casa de La Cacha*, the house of the "fat woman", who sold it to the man whose son sold it to me. Now, of course, they call it *la casa del inglé*, the Englishman's house, but for the rest of mankind, it is *El Cortijo de los Siete Olivos*.

La Cacha's real name was Catalina and she grew up a stone's throw down the hill in her father's house. Her sad distinction was that she was an unwed mother, which in those days was tantamount to being a "fallen woman". The neighbours tell me that while working as a housekeeper for a land-owner across the valley she was made pregnant by the man's son and sent home in disgrace. This was seen as a great tragedy, in spite of the fact that Catalina was already some forty years old. Her father refused to take his daughter back in the family home, but in her condition couldn't put her in the street either, so he gave her the other house which stood on his land, just up the hill. He even insisted on drawing up a deed in her name, as if to erect a "wall of shame" around her, cutting a piece off from the rest of his property. That is why the house stands on such an unusually small plot, which, in turn, is why I could afford to buy it.

There are two things about which the normally hard-bitten Spanish peasants are especially unsentimental: one, as I have learned over the years, is anything even remotely related to sex, and the other is water. Catalina's father went so far as to stipulate that she could only use the water which filled her small aljibe, from an ancient underground channel, for domestic purposes rather than irrigation, and that she should allow the overflow, or *derrame*, to continue on down, where he used it to water his orchard at the bottom of the hill. There is a clause in the deeds of both houses which was inherited from this curious arrangement, according to which the *aljibe* itself does not belong to me but, rather, to the man who bought it from the heirs of Catalina's unforgiving father. But the notary assures me that such "home-made" clauses ("I hereby sell you this field but I retain the right to graze my donkey on it from March to June...") were common in the times when an *escritura* was often just a bit of paper signed with thumbprints, and that due to their irrational nature they never stand up in court.

Catalina made a living by raising chickens and selling the eggs in the market. I often imagine the suffering, between these walls, without solar-powered light bulbs or butane-burning refrigerator, of the unmarried woman alone with her unwanted child; but my bricklayer and the passing shepherd prefer to remember the good times they had here as young men, which may well have included visits under cover of darkness. This is precisely why the local ladies looked down on Catalina as a *marrana*, or slut - a woman without a husband was a threat to every Christian household. But all of them, respectable *señoras* included, used to enjoy the *bailes* which Catalina gave to make some extra money. My neighbour Alfonso fondly recalls how someone would always bring along an accordion or a guitar so that the neighhourhood swains could steer the marriageable *mozuelas*, at less than arm's length if they dared, through a rasping pasodoble, here in the same raftered room where I am now writing, on my computer, by the fire.

I am told that her son, Celestino, is now the father of no less than twelve children of his own, and lives in another farm near the road to Alcalá. Catalina moved out when he married, in the early 60's, and ended her days almost a centenarian, at a relative's home near Puerto Lope. She sold the house to a field labourer whose nickname was Morcón (*morcón* is a kind of sausage), who 20 years later was killed in the stable (now the downstairs bedroom) by a mule, which reared up and drove an iron yolk into his chest. His widow and children immediately moved away and put the house up for sale. Perhaps it was because they superstitiously wanted to be rid of it that they asked for so little - less, in fact, than what I paid for the second-hand *dos caballos* delivery van which I had just bought from Pedro Romero. To paraphrase an old saying, the desire for money is great, but the fear of death is even greater...

As the name indicates, the cortijo is surrounded with seven olive trees, as well as ten almond trees, two fig trees, one pomegranate, one quince tree, and a *chumbera*, or fig-cactus. I thought that the "Farm of the Seven Olive Trees" sounded romantic, but to the villagers the name seems laughably modest, since any self-respecting *finca* has at least several hundred of the precious plants, not just seven.

I had no idea of how to build, of where plaster should be used and where cement, or how a door or window frame were installed or pipes were laid, so I hired one of Rocio's student friends, who was studying to be an architect, to help me direct the six workers who were to make the place suitable for semi-civilized summertime living. But even resourceful José could not protect me from all the "unforeseeables".

As soon as we began work, the venerable *venero* proved to be a springtime-only affair and ran dry, so that for the next six weeks (which was exactly three times as long as my workers assured me the whole operation would take), I had to shuttle three or four 200-litre tanks of water a day down the bumpy road, from a fountain two miles away. Pedro Romero's *furgoneta* heroically managed to get me back to Paris by the time winter set in, but there it was diagnosed by a Belleville mechanic as *foutue* and sold for scrap. It simply never occurred to me that construction requires not only plaster and cement, but, also, lots and lots of water.

We built a fireplace like a great white toadstool to replace the painted flat one, a kitchen where the main bedroom had been (the house had none - they cooked in a hut outdoors); we bored through the 2-foot thick walls to make windows for the somber rooms and created an extension to house the bathroom which, in that already distant year of 1985, was the largest in Montefrio at 9 square metres - with a family-sized tub, thought to be somewhat fanciful for a house which had no supply of water... We rebuilt the long porch, which had collapsed, and covered the granite floor tiles with brick-red *catalanas*. But by the end of a seemingly endless summer of dust, heat and sweating workmen - who never missed a chance to let me know that they thought I was mad for not tearing the whole thing down and building a snappy new *chalé* - I was so fed up that I wished I had never had the idea of buying a house in the first place.

But when I returned to Spain the following spring, I had forgotten all that and discovered, for the first time, the thrill of having a house of my own, a place on which I had left my own personal imprint. It was, and is, like a second skin, without which I now feel strangely naked. And the view from the porch of Parapanda Mountain was so beautiful that I could scarcely tear myself away from my deck chair, especially when the setting sun made it glow as if it had been baked in a kiln. However, I had already made plans to visit old friends in Brazil, and a few months later was off again.

It was three years before I returned to live in my house, in the company of a handsome young Brazilian woman and our chubby brown baby girl, Nina. From then on - the summer of 1989 - I set about making it suitable for permanent residence.

This began with water. The chances of digging a well with an adequate year-round supply of water seemed so small, from what the locals told me, that I audaciously decided to lay over one mile of black PVC pipe and hook up to the village water system. This required having a steam shovel dig a metre-deep trench across several olive groves, after getting the owners' authorization. The whole operation cost me more than the original price of the house, and there was no guarantee that it would work, since Montefrio's water supply (initially pumped from a deep well in the mountains) comes from a holding tank on the hill above the village, from which it "falls" down by force of gravity alone. Since my house is almost as high as this holding tank, and several miles away with numerous ups and downs in between, I could only guess, from visual sightings using a carpenter's level attached to a long metal rod, that the difference in level - four or five meters at the most - would be sufficient for the flow to reach the top of my own reserve tank on the roof of the house. I will never forget the day my father and I held up the black pipe to the required height and saw a sluggish, but sufficiently voluminous flow of water come out of the end, making me our water company's highest situated and furthest removed customer.

There seemed to be little chance of getting hooked up to the local electrical grid, because my farm is the only inhabited house for several kilometers around and a transformer just for me would be extremely costly. So I acquired four photovoltaic panels, a couple of car batteries and a set of 12 volt incandescent lights, as well as a petrol generator for rainy days and electrical appliances. Sometimes I joke that the farm should be called the cortijo of the twelve volts! It all costs me a great deal in burned-out batteries and fuel, but it allows me to live comfortably where I want to be... Since the mile of dirt road turns to mud after a few minutes of rain, I purchased a small Russian-made land vehicle which can crawl over any amount of damage caused by landslides and flash floods, and up almost anything but the olive trees themselves.

The telephone was my greatest concern, since I was planning to resume work as a free-lance translator and interpreter, after a prolonged sabbatical. I put in my petition to the rural installation department in Granada, where I was told that I would spend several years on the waiting list. While there I happened to make friends with the refined, spinsterly type in charge who, in the course of the conversation, declared herself greatly interested in my pen and ink drawings. I invited her to lunch at a nearby restaurant so that we could look at them together, and I was soon invited to her flat in return to see her watercolours. Maria Carmen never mentioned my installation again, so I was amazed, a few months later, to find a team of men erecting a row of 22 telephone poles leading straight across the olive groves to my little house. What's more, the dear lady saw to it that I did not have to pay for a single one of them.

cortijo

La Villa as it was when I first saw it in 1960, without the pine forest or the tiled roof on the bell tower.

Also as it was then, the high part of Montefrío called El Coro. The Calvary Chapel is in the upper right, with three white crosses of the Vía Crucis leading to it. When Manolo took me there to sing flamenco with the gypsies, I saw they still lived in thatched huts covered with retama, *or broom.*

*La Cruz Gorda on the road to El Tocón,
with La Villa in the background...*

Author Lawrence Bohme was born in London in 1942 to an English mother and a German war refugee father, spending his first years "under Hitler's rockets". When he was 4, the family emigrated to Vancouver, where Lawrence "failed to become a real Canadian boy, but loved the trees". 10 years later his restless and beautiful mother decided to abandon home and husband to become a painter in Mexico, where Lawrence learned his first foreign language and became a bullfight aficionado, "a passion which, like so many others, has long since faded". After several years they moved to Jamaica, still under British rule, where Lawrence discovered his "first tropical paradise and the beauty of the island girls". By the time he was 16 his mother had led him to Greenwich Village which was where he was "really born". It is significant, perhaps, that his surname "Bohme" was originally spelled "Böhme" (but anglicized during the war, when having a German name was undesirable) which means "man from the old state of Bohemia", or simply put, "bohemian".

At age 18, Lawrence set out, on his own this time, to "be a student, rather than really study, at the University of Madrid, a thrilling experience of no academic worth", soon ending up in an Andalucian village near Granada called Montefrio, where he had befriended an eccentric flamenco singer, Manuel Avila, who was also the town butcher, and where he was christened "Lorenzo" by the locals, "a name that stuck so well that when my hair went white they began calling me Don Lorenzo". Hooking up with a "temperamental and self-destructive" German painter he met in the streets of Granada, Lilo, Lawrence moved to Paris to study at the Sorbonne, where, in his words, he "learned many important things", one of which was that he "didn't want to spend any more time in schools". Tiring of both Lilo and Paris, he drifted aimlessly about Rome and Sicily "for one long autumn, admiring the frescoes and façades" before "returning home" to New York. There, he fell in love with Virginia, "the Panamanian voodoo doll", and "after seeing the film Black Orpheus 16 times also fell in love with Brazilian music and women", making his way there a few years later, on a Japanese freighter carrying immigrants from Yokohama to Rio de Janeiro, via Los Angeles.

His long stay in Rio, where he lived in a favela with a fisherman and his family and became a leather bag and sandal maker, "was both exciting and illuminating", but at the end of five years he had "another fit of wanderlust" and, after some wanderings, found himself in the Haiti of "Baby Doc" Duvalier, teaching sugar cane cutters to sew leather satchels which he exported to men's fashion shops on Lexington Avenue and St. Marks Place. Having learned creole and explored the hills of southern Haiti on the back of a small white horse he called "Blanc", he "fell out with the local *ton-ton macoutes*" and, now in the company of his adventurous mother, fled to Cartagena, Colombia where he set up another leather shop.

From there began an odyssey through the Caribbean islands, making leather bags and drawing pen-and-ink postcards "to keep body and soul together": San Andres, Grand Cayman, Saint Martin and Saint Barths. For reasons too complicated to describe here, he returned to Europe in 1981, living in a village high in the hills of Provence and then Paris, where he had his greatest success as a postcard designer and became an external translator for Unesco, "at last working in a field I was originally educated for, to my dear old Dad's great relief". A few years later, Lawrence returned to his beloved Andalucian town, Montefrio, where he bought a white house in the olive trees and "began studying history in earnest, because – unless you want to become a dentist or an astronomer - it's the only thing worth studying".

An unforeseen return visit to Rio resulted in the birth of his daughter Nina, who along with her mother accompanied him back to Montefrio and Granada. There, Lawrence made his living as a simultaneous interpreter at conferences around Spain, while restoring several cottages which he rented to visitors as "Las Casas de Lorenzo".

After an impetuous incursion into village politics "at the risk of my life", Lawrence, a bachelor again, moved to Granada's old casbah, the Albaicin. There he began writing about his life and travels "in the company of a daring Moorish girl" who in 2005 gave him "a son, August, named for my father and great-great grandfather".

WRST SE
EX13 SNX

Printed in Great Britain
by Amazon

83857177R00078